Practical Strategies for Supporting Emotional
Regulation in Students with Autism

PRACTICAL STRATEGIES FOR SUPPORTING EMOTIONAL REGULATION IN STUDENTS WITH AUTISM

Enhancing Engagement and Learning in the Classroom

LESLIE BLOME

with MAUREEN ZELLE

Jessica Kingsley *Publishers*
London and Philadelphia

Picture symbols used in photographs are reproduced with permission from
The Picture Communication Symbols © 1981-2015 by Mayer-Johnson
LCC a Tobii Dynavox company. All Rights Reserved Worldwide.

First published in 2018
by Jessica Kingsley Publishers
73 Collier Street
London N1 9BE, UK
and
400 Market Street, Suite 400
Philadelphia, PA 19106, USA

www.jkp.com

Library of Congress Cataloging in Publication Data
A CIP catalog record for this book is available from the Library of Congress

British Library Cataloguing in Publication Data
A CIP catalogue record for this book is available from the British Library

ISBN 978 1 78592 778 2
eISBN 978 1 78450 690 2

Printed and bound by CPI Group (UK) Ltd, Croydon, CR0 4YY

CONTENTS

ONE MORE THING

ACKNOWLEDGEMENTS

We extend our deepest gratitude to the mentors who guided and encouraged us, the families who trusted us, and the students with autism who challenged us and brought us joy.

Thank you, also, to the group of witty, talented, tender-hearted women who comprised our team during the writing of this book: Terri, Melaina, Emily, Tammy, Kim, Aittqa, and Carrie.

Leslie and Mo

Thank you to my son, Matthew, for your patience, encouragement, and love.

Mo

Thank you to my sons, Liam, Aidan, and Kieran, who have enriched my life immeasurably. Finally, my heartfelt gratitude to my husband, Jon, whose love and support enabled me to write this book—every day with you is a gift.

Leslie

INTRODUCTION

CHARACTERISTICS OF AUTISM

Autism spectrum disorder (ASD) is a developmental disorder that is characterized by impaired social interaction and restricted, repetitive patterns of behavior (American Psychiatric Association, 2013). Individuals with autism process information differently to neurotypical individuals, which affects their ability to understand and communicate with others and impacts the way they relate to people and objects in their environment (Janzen and Zenko, 2012; Rydell, 2012). The wide variation in severity of symptoms and level of intellectual functioning, and the presence of co-occurring conditions, cause ASD to look very different from one person to another. The prevalence of autism has risen dramatically in recent years. Current worldwide incidence is estimated to be 1:160 (World Health Organization, 2017), while incidence in the United States is reportedly 1:68 (Center for Disease Control and Prevention, 2016). Males are much more likely to be diagnosed with ASD than females. However, there is increasing awareness that the symptoms of autism may manifest differently in girls, increasing the likelihood that they might be overlooked using current diagnostic parameters (Gould and Ashton-Smith, 2011).

EMOTIONAL REGULATION

The pattern of challenges and characteristics experienced by individuals with ASD makes it difficult for them to stay emotionally regulated. As an internal process, emotional regulation enables a person to maintain a well-regulated emotional state to cope with everyday stress and to be most available for learning and interacting (Prizant and Laurent, 2011a). It is a foundational skill that underlies attention, social engagement, and communication development (Prizant and Meyer, 1993). According to Prizant *et al.* (2006), emotional regulation is associated with the ability to maintain an optimal state of arousal for learning. Students with autism have significant difficulty modulating their level of arousal. Some may tend toward frequent states of high arousal, resulting in extreme reactions to feelings of anxiety, distress, and even elation (Prizant *et al.*, 2006). Other students on the spectrum may appear passive, as they tend toward frequent states of low arousal (Prizant *et al.*, 2006). In either of these states, the student is considered dysregulated and is consequently unavailable for learning and interacting.

As professionals who work with students on the autism spectrum in an inclusive preschool setting, our primary responsibility is to support our students so that they can stay emotionally regulated. We want to help them spend as much time as possible within the range of optimal arousal so that they can interact and learn. We have found that the time and attention we devote to determining which strategies will help our students stay emotionally regulated pays dividends in the subsequent learning that takes place. Everything we do has the goal of enhancing engagement and learning.

Over the years, we have compiled a large bank of strategies that we can utilize to support the emotional regulation of our students. Of course, our end goal is for our students to develop self-regulation skills. We want them to learn to monitor their own arousal state and independently employ strategies to stay regulated. However, because we work with young students who are significantly impacted, we typically spend most of our time teaching our students to respond to our assistance to achieve mutual regulation (Prizant *et al.*, 2006). Based on our knowledge of and experience with each student, we begin with the strategies that we think will work best. However, the preschool classroom is a dynamic environment. Social and cognitive demands are constantly shifting, and the student with autism may become dysregulated as he struggles to adapt his emotional responses in relation to internal states and external demands (Prizant *et al.*, 2006). Students on the autism spectrum often have difficulty adapting given rigid thinking patterns, difficulty processing sensory input, social-communicative deficits, and other challenges (Prizant *et al.*, 2006). As educators, we need to be as dynamic as our preschool classrooms, ready to employ alternative strategies as the students' needs and behaviors shift and change.

It is important to mention that emotional regulation is not just a skill for students on the autism spectrum. All students, and in fact all people, need to maintain a state of emotional regulation to be present for learning and coping with change. The ability to stay regulated, which is more problematic for some individuals than others, evolves slowly over time (Lowry, 2016). It enables one to "focus when there are distractions, pay attention to the most important information, take turns, wait, follow rules, adapt to new situations, do what is socially expected, suppress outbursts of anger, and take on challenges" (Lowry, 2016). Clearly, learning to regulate oneself is one of the primary tasks of childhood.

While it is true that students exhibiting characteristics of typical neurological development, or neurotypical students, are generally more adept at the difficult task of staying regulated than students on the autism spectrum, we can and do use regulation strategies successfully with all the students in our classroom. For example, it is not uncommon for us to need to alter our daily classroom schedule. We might need to eliminate outside time due to weather. A student with autism might respond to this unexpected change in the routine by becoming dysregulated and beginning to tantrum or cry. A neurotypical student would likely be able to stay calm, process the change, and move on. However, we have certainly seen typically developing students who reacted to a change by becoming dysregulated, thus requiring additional support and strategies.

Similarly, our guidelines and strategies are certainly not exclusive to the preschool classroom setting. They can easily be adapted for use in the home or community, as well as throughout the lifespan. We have helped many parents learn to use the strategies with their students at home and in the community. For example, using a contingency statement (e.g. "*First* grocery store/ *Then* park") and showing the student a list of the items that must be bought ("Show how many") might help a family make a successful trip to the grocery store. These same strategies could help an older student or adult with autism wait in line or complete a non-preferred work task. As you read through our guidelines and strategies, consider how they might be used in different settings and with varying populations.

The combination of the ten "cognitive/language strategies" we will outline, together with a multitude of sensory strategies and our underlying "Three Guidelines," provide us with a treasure trove of supports to use to help our students stay regulated.[1] We look at each new day as a challenge, knowing that a strategy that worked yesterday might not work today. We must constantly shift, collaborate, and think creatively to meet the needs of our students in the dynamic classroom environment. When we do this successfully, we get the joy of watching our students stay regulated and available for learning and engagement.

OUR APPROACH

Our approach is an integrated one. Although our ideology is most closely tied to developmental/relationship-based models, it also has elements of positive behavior support and structured teaching. We also take into consideration the student's ability to process his environment given his sensory systems, as well as physiological states and social factors (Janzen and Zenko, 2012). It has been our experience that the success of our students depends on our willingness to apply an integrated approach. We believe that each student with autism is unique in terms of his constellation of autism characteristics, his sensory profile, his personality, and more. Accordingly, each student will need a distinctive program to achieve regulation and learning. In addition to providing a multi-faceted approach to working with our students, other guiding principles that contribute to our approach include: gain trust, collaborate, seek to understand behavior, find balance, and adapt.

---

1   The SCERTS Model (Prizant *et al.*, 2006) uses the terms "cognitive strategies" and "language strategies" separately, but not in combination. We use the term "cognitive/language strategies" as a descriptor to distinguish these strategies from the bank of sensory strategies that we use.

Gain Trust

We believe, first and foremost, that we must form positive, nurturing relationships with our students. We must gain their trust. A student will not respond to the strategies that we are using if he does not trust us. That is the bottom line. We have found that our ability to positively affect a student's behavior increases when we have established a warm and trusting relationship, a finding that is supported in the literature (Fox *et al.*, 2003; Joseph and Strain, 2004). One of the most frequent comments we receive upon the conclusion of our presentations, which are filled with video footage of us working with our students, is, "We can really see how much you love these kids." This is so evident because we have true affection and respect for our students and genuinely enjoy interacting with each one. The process of connecting with each student is one of the most rewarding parts of our job.

Collaborate

Prizant *et al.* (2006) cite inefficient teaming as one barrier to providing quality programs for students with ASD. Preconceived notions about how a classroom should run, and what each professional's role should entail, can quickly impede collaboration. Just as we work to form a fun and trusting relationship with our kids, we strive to do that with each other and our staff, as well. We are extremely fortunate to have a team that works together cooperatively, with each person doing whatever needs to be done in the moment. When others have come into our classroom for trainings, they often comment on this. It doesn't matter that we all have separate job descriptions—Early Childhood Special Educator (ECSE), Speech-Language Pathologist (SLP), classroom teacher, Occupational Therapist (OT), aide—everyone just does what needs to be done. Any of us might be found using strategies to bring a student back from the edge of dysregulation, working 1:1 on requesting, changing a diaper, or setting the table for snack. Keeping the common goal of helping our students at the forefront of our minds keeps us all moving in the same direction. What's more, you will almost always find us having fun. Truthfully, this can be a very stressful job. We have some very difficult students who need us to be vigilant—mentally and physically. Joking with each other helps us stay on top of our game mentally. We want to come to work every day, not only for the students, but for each other as well.

Finally, we place the utmost importance on collaborating with parents and forming good working relationships. Parents are the ones who know their children best. They also spend *much* more time with their children than we do. We need to team with parents not only to provide consistency for our students across settings, but also to increase dramatically the amount of time each child is actively engaged. Many programs that employ a strictly behavioural approach assert that students with autism need 20–45 hours of intervention per week. However, the National Research Council (2001) actually specifies 25 or more hours per week of *active engagement*. This is much easier to achieve when parents feel supported and are well-versed in methods to keep their children regulated and engaged.

Seek to Understand Behavior

Problem behavior—that which interferes with learning, engaging and forming relationships—is often an attempt to regulate arousal level or simply the "outward expression of an inward state" (Janzen and Zenko, 2012, p.104). Other times, the student's behavior is an attempt to communicate or a habituated response to a specific environmental situation (Janzen and Zenko, 2012). For students with autism, dysregulation is often the genesis of challenging behavior (Prizant and Laurent, 2011b). Instead of attempting to simply stop difficult behavior, we view it from a framework of understanding the cause of the behavior and how dysregulation fits into the picture. Once we understand the underlying cause or motivation for the behavior, we can provide the necessary supports to help the student cope. Not only that, but we can also prevent problem behavior altogether by decreasing the frequency, duration, and intensity of dysregulation. Employing prevention strategies, in the form of emotional regulatory supports throughout the student's day, is the primary way we do this.

Find Balance

In working with our students, we constantly strive to find a balance between challenging them to move to the next level—pushing them just enough in terms of communication and flexibility—and gauging the appropriateness of the demand so that they do not become overwhelmed and dysregulated. This is an intricate dance—and we don't always get it right. Not only that, but we must also constantly monitor the emotional regulation capacity of each student (The SCERTS Model, 2017). As educators in an inclusive classroom, where our students are integrated almost 100 percent of the time, the environment is a constant. We must provide the support each student needs to learn and derive meaning from *this* experience. We are absolutely proponents of inclusion and all its advantages, and we are also aware of the challenges that this presents for some of our students.

We also strive to strike a balance between following the student's lead and requiring him to follow ours. We believe in building upon each student's interests and strengths to tap into his internal motivation to engage and interact. We want our students to experience some social control to help them remain regulated and motivated. We also understand that to do this all the time would be a disservice to our students. Students with autism, like all people, need to learn that sometimes others will follow their lead and also that they must frequently follow the agenda of others. This is the reality of living in our world, and it is a lifelong theme. As humans, our ability to embrace flexibility profoundly affects our interactions with others. This flexibility, sometimes called "shared control" (Koegel and Koegel, 2006; Rydell, 2012), can be particularly difficult for our students. It can be a significant barrier to participating and engaging with others successfully. If we can make some progress toward helping our students overcome this limitation, it will serve them in the years to come.

Adapt

Finally, we must be flexible ourselves. We are extremely consistent with students regarding our expectation that they follow through on instructions once they are issued and on tasks until they are completed. We must be flexible and creative, though, in the manner of support we provide to assist the student in doing this. We are aware that often (not just sometimes—often) the strategy we are using will not work. Despite the numerous preventative strategies that are consistently in place in our classroom (e.g. visual schedules, choice-making opportunities, sensory accommodations, etc.) (Prizant and Laurent, 2011b), dysregulation occurs regularly. At any given moment, upon entering our classroom, you may see dysregulation in action. It might look like rolling on the floor, screaming, laughing uncontrollably, or staring into space. Whatever the case, that student is not available to learn.

What you will also see is one of our team using a strategy, or combination of strategies, to help bring the student back to a state of regulation where he is available for learning and engagement. And if that strategy is not working, you will see us assessing the situation, trying to understand the reason for the dysregulation from the student's point of view, and analyzing our own contribution to the interaction. We may determine that it is appropriate to hold our ground and continue with the strategy we are using, perhaps tweaking our approach just a bit. If not, we may begin running through our strategies to determine which one might help him in this situation. It might be that the strategy we are currently using worked yesterday—or even five minutes ago—but if it is not working now, we may need to adapt. Something is different for the student, so it is our job to find what will work in this moment. And we may need to shift and change our approach tomorrow, too. We have come to expect this, which enables us to adapt quickly and without frustration or confusion. It doesn't surprise us when what we are doing doesn't work, and we don't take it personally. And when a student is having a full-blown meltdown, it doesn't necessarily mean we've done something wrong; it just means we need to re-assess and find a different way to support that student right now.

OUR BOOK

For the past four years, we have collaborated in an inclusive preschool classroom to design and implement the programs for students on the autism spectrum deemed "high needs." Working with this population in this type of setting dictates that we spend much of our time supporting our students so that they can stay regulated. As we combined our skills and knowledge, we discovered that we had quite a large collection of strategies that worked with our students. We mentored our own team not only regarding when and how to use these strategies with the students, but also *why* we use them. We discovered that we had something that was useful to other professionals. We began to give presentations locally, as well as at national conferences. We also began to demonstrate our strategies in our own classroom, as colleagues within our early childhood department signed up to come and observe and participate in our classroom for a day.

As the incidence of autism has risen, more and more professionals have students with autism on their caseload. Many report that they feel unprepared to support these students in the classroom. Others report that they know some strategies but are unsure of what to do when those strategies don't work. Still others report that they have been using some of the strategies for years, without knowing *why* they were using them. Many professionals know basic information about autism but have not had specific training in how to respond to the behaviors exhibited—behaviors that can be disruptive and that can seem arbitrary and incongruous. It can be frustrating and confusing when one doesn't have the background to interpret these behaviors or the tools to respond productively. The feedback we have received indicates that these colleagues are hungry for practical strategies that they can use in their classrooms. Not only that, they also want to know *why* each strategy works. Understanding the rationale behind the strategies increases effectiveness and independence, as it allows each professional to adapt the strategies as students' needs shift and change.

Following our presentations and classroom trainings, many of our colleagues requested additional resources on the strategies we spoke about and demonstrated. As we scoured the literature, we indeed found many similar strategies, but they were either buried within text that delved deeply into theory and research, in sources that went into great detail about one type of strategy, or in workbooks or articles that listed several strategies but did not provide theoretical background information (the *why*). These are all necessary and useful formats for presenting what has been discovered about working with students on the spectrum. That said, professionals have large caseloads and busy lives—they need practical strategies that they can use immediately to help their students with autism stay regulated and ready to learn. They also want to be knowledgeable about the research and theory behind what they are doing with their students. Our book is an effort to provide a single, easily accessible resource that provides practical strategies paired with brief summaries of the rationale and research that support them.

This book is by no means an attempt to exhaust all possible strategies for teaching students with autism in an inclusive classroom. Nor is it meant to present all the available research behind these strategies. It is a practical guide to using the guidelines and strategies that we have found successful over the years. Each chapter gives the reader a brief overview of the research behind one strategy, followed by a detailed description of how we implement the strategy in the classroom. At the end of each chapter, several examples of the strategy in action are provided, so the reader can get a clear picture of how it can be implemented. Following the strategy chapters, there is a chapter devoted to describing some techniques we use—little details of how we interact with our students—that increase the effectiveness of the strategies. Finally, several helpful appendices are included, including one that lays out sample situations and cross-references how each of our strategies might be implemented in the given situation.

Our sincere wish is that our colleagues find this book helpful. We hope that it enhances each professional's ability to work with students on the autism spectrum effectively and with confidence, in the classroom and beyond.

CHAPTER 1

THREE GUIDELINES

During the process of organizing our strategies to share with our colleagues, we discovered that there are three strategies that are more pervasive than the others. We use these three overarching strategies—by themselves and in conjunction with more specific ones—every time we interact with a student. We decided to call these three strategies our "Guidelines." When a student begins to become dysregulated, we find that it is extremely helpful to start by doing a mental check to ensure that we have employed these guidelines during the interaction. If not, we implement any missing Guideline(s) immediately. This is sometimes enough to get the student back on the road to regulation. The Three Guidelines are:

- Provide processing time

- Use simple language

- Employ visuals.

PROVIDE PROCESSING TIME

As adults, when a student with autism is not responding to a request, direction, or communication, our tendency is to want to help. We often assume that because the student does not respond right away, he does not know what to do. We may quickly jump in and answer for him, give additional prompts, or tell him what to do. Although our intentions are good—we want to help—the outcome is not a positive one for the student. The student becomes accustomed to this behavior and learns to wait for the extra cues and instructions. He becomes prompt-dependent.

It is well documented in the literature that students with ASD typically need more processing time than their peers. Time is needed to process the auditory information, interpret the nonverbal social cues, and determine how to respond (Hodgdon, 1991; Prizant *et al.*, 2006). Giving the student time to move through these steps not only decreases frustration levels (thus increasing regulation), but also ensures that the student has the chance to do the thinking for himself (Rydell, 2012). For the sake of the student's regulation, learning, and independence, we need to learn to wait. We need to wait longer than is comfortable for us. The simple act of waiting yields amazing results time after time. There is a dramatic increase in what a student can process and execute given time. It is incredibly important that we learn to wait so that each student has the opportunity to develop these skills.

Consider your own reaction to being rushed. When you are trying to process something that is challenging for you, it increases your anxiety when you are not given the time to do so. Furthermore, think about how dysregulating it is when another person then jumps in and answers for you or completes the task just as you are about to do it. As a neurotypical adult, you may be able to identify your emotions in the moment and cope with them in a way that is acceptable in the social situation. For several reasons, a student with autism, especially a young one, will likely not be able to do that. As professionals working with students on the autism spectrum, it is our responsibility to determine the amount of processing time each individual student typically requires—and then provide it. The benefits of allowing ample processing time will be twofold: increased regulation and decreased prompt-dependency.

USE SIMPLE LANGUAGE

Keeping language simple and direct aids comprehension and helps the student with ASD to focus on the essential parts of our message. We need to use language that is concise and specific, while eliminating words that don't give relevant information. It is especially important to use simple language in the classroom setting (where distractions are abundant) and when the student is becoming dysregulated. As therapists and teachers, when a student is having a difficult time following through on a task or instruction, our natural inclination is to talk more. Whether the intention is to convince the student to participate, provide assistance by "talking him through it," or ease our own anxiety, our rate of speech tends to increase. For example, a student might be starting to have a meltdown over hanging up his backpack, and we might find ourselves saying, "Come on, Kevin. Hang up your backpack. Right here! You can do it. Pick it up. Here, let me help you." As our anxiety increases, not only do we talk faster, but our pitch and volume may increase, as well. This is natural and difficult to counteract.

However, this verbosity can quickly become counter-productive, especially for a student with autism. We need to re-program ourselves to communicate in a way that will help our student recognize and understand the salient features of our message. We need to distill our language down to the essential message—and then just say those words. For example:

> "Time to wash hands. Let's go. Wash your hands in the big sink. Come on," *becomes* "Wash hands," with a point toward the big sink and wait time.

> "We are going outside. Let's put on our coats. Coats on, line up by the door," *becomes* "Coat on, then line up," with a point toward the coat rack and wait time.

> "Circle time. Let's go sit at circle. Time for story. Sit on your carpet square," *becomes* "Your friends are sitting," with a point toward the children sitting at circle and wait time.

We must also remember that we need to *stop talking* altogether once we have stated the message clearly and simply. This goes together with providing processing time and is especially important when the student is under tension or when a response is required on his part (Janzen and Zenko, 2012).

Using simple language is not only crucial when a student is already becoming dysregulated, it is also important as a preventive measure. Getting in the habit of using simple, direct language during transitions and other high-stress times can sometimes preclude dysregulation from occurring in the first place. Of course, it is extremely important to address the language skills of our students through language expansion techniques and modeling, but now is not the time to do it. We may model and elicit more sophisticated language during those times when our student is not at risk of becoming dysregulated—when he is calm and available for learning and interacting. We can often keep students on the spectrum regulated and prevent meltdowns altogether by stating expectations and instructions clearly, firmly, and with simple language.

Again, consider your own needs at times when you feel overwhelmed or confused. When someone continues to talk at you, it becomes more and more distressing. You need time to process the message, take stock of your own emotions, and decide how you will proceed. This is a complicated process. For the student with autism, consider that he may already be in a state of heightened anxiety and most likely has difficulty processing language to some degree. Simplifying your language and providing the time to process that language can go a long way toward helping him stay regulated and ready to learn!

The next time you are interacting with a student on the spectrum and you see his anxiety begin to increase, think about exactly what he needs to do and say it in a few words. State the expectation firmly and clearly, adding a gesture where needed and plenty of wait time. Speak a little more slowly than usual, and use pauses and vocal stress to emphasize especially important words (Janzen and Zenko, 2012). Stay calm yourself, and let your tone of voice and manner of speaking reflect this. Your quiet state will anchor the student and help quell his anxiety. Remember: stay calm, be firm, and use precise language. Once you do this enough, it will start to become second nature, and your students will reap the benefits.

EMPLOY VISUALS

Visualization plays a significant role in language comprehension for students with ASD (Kana *et al.*, 2006). There is substantial evidence in the literature that students on the autism spectrum manage more effectively and learn more readily when given visual information as opposed to solely verbal information (Hodgdon, 1991; Quill, 1997; Schuler, 1995). Visual supports, especially those that stay accessible long enough for adequate processing to occur (Mesibov, Shea, and Schopler, 2004), can dramatically improve comprehension. Furthermore, when we use visual supports, we are teaching to a relative strength for our students (Hodgdon, 1999). Hodgdon (1999) divides visual supports into three categories including using: yourself (e.g. gestures, facial expressions); items that are already present in the environment (e.g. objects, signs, people); tools created specifically to meet the needs of our students (e.g. visual schedules, choice boards).

Gestures and facial expressions are a more transient form of visual support, given that, like verbalizations, they vanish after the interaction. Nevertheless, they are a quick, clear way to support comprehension. When interacting with our students, we consistently use our bodies to provide visual support. Looking expectant, pointing, and gesturing toward an object are all visual tools. Often, we simply move our whole bodies near what we want the student to attend to, make a sound (such as a throat clear), and wait. This is a more indirect way of providing a visual support and can sometimes be enough to get the job done. We are aware that, even when providing a visual prompt with our bodies, there are varying levels of prompting. The level of support increases as we progress through directing the student's attention using our whole body, to gesturing with our arm/hand (no pointing), to using a distal point and finally a contact point. We always strive to use the least directive level of prompting that is required, thus encouraging the student to think independently.

The use of objects and picture visuals, whether already in the environment or uniquely created, allows for the provision of adequate processing time. The student can continue to process the idea while the picture or object is in front of him, as contrasted with a verbalization that vanishes as soon as it is spoken. This gives the student time to shift his attention, engage, and process the message before it is gone (Hodgdon, 1995).

Whenever possible, we provide visuals at the appropriate level of iconicity (e.g. object, photo, line drawing) to support comprehension. We utilize visuals so frequently during the day that we have pockets of them posted throughout the classroom. This enables us to provide a visual quickly and efficiently as soon as we recognize that a student needs visual support to process what is coming next or to move away from his own agenda.

Of course, we use visuals proactively in our classroom, as well. The whole classroom is visually organized for all students in terms of the space, as well as the schedule of the day. Visual cues are used routinely to let students know where to stand in line, indicate boundaries when sitting, and to let students know how many individuals can be in a center/ activity area at one time. Many of our students with ASD also have individual schedules for the daily routine and/or to structure particularly challenging portions of the day. The use of visuals to indicate what is happening now, as well as what happens next (Mesibov *et al.*, 2004), is extremely important to the flow of the classroom and all our students' independence, not only those with autism.

◼ EXAMPLE

It is the beginning of the school day, and the students are coming into the classroom. The first step of the daily arrival routine is for each student to hang his backpack on his hook. Although he has the skills to do this independently, your student is refusing and is sitting on the floor and beginning to whine. Given that arrival time is a major transition, you will want to have a visual schedule of the arrival routine posted where it can be seen easily. We post ours with Velcro, so that we have the option of handing it to the student, holding it where he can see it better, or setting it down next to him.

You start by calling the student's attention to the visual schedule by tapping it with your hand. Point to the picture of the backpack if necessary. *Wait*, look expectant, and shift your gaze from the child's backpack to the hook. If he does not respond, repeat this sequence and add simple language, "backpack." You may be tempted to talk more and tell the student how to proceed. Instead, wait ten more seconds and look expectant. If he still doesn't do it, tap the hook and look from the backpack to the hook, and *wait* again. While you are waiting, stay near the student and stay alert to his actions, but avoid watching him intently. When you look elsewhere, and perhaps briefly give some attention to other things that are happening nearby, you give your student the space to respond on his own. You may need to wait quite a while, but be sure to gauge the student's body language to ensure that he is still engaged and focused on the task at hand.

Employing the Three Guidelines in the manner described above may be enough support to help your student stay regulated and move on. If not, additional strategies, which will be discussed in the forthcoming chapters, may be necessary.

THREE GUIDELINES

Use *every time* you interact with a student**

Provide Processing Time

- ✓ Wait, wait, *wait*
- ✓ Monitor student engagement
- ✓ Determine processing time for each student

Use Simple Language

- ✓ Use language that is precise and direct
- ✓ *Stop talking* once the message has been stated
- ✓ Use pauses to separate your message
- ✓ Emphasize important words

Employ Visuals

- ✓ Exaggerate facial expressions
- ✓ Use body placement and gestures
- ✓ Call attention to objects, photos, and line drawings
- ✓ Create student-specific visuals for challenging activities and portions of the day

CHAPTER 2

SENSORY OVERVIEW

Although our book is specifically about the cognitive/language strategies we use, it is important to mention that we also employ many sensory strategies. A high proportion of students with autism have sensory processing difficulties. In fact, one study found that approximately 78 percent of students with autism also exhibited symptoms of sensory processing disorder (SPD) (Miller, 2014). Sensory processing is the process in which "our brains receive sensory information from our bodies and surroundings, interprets these messages, and organize our purposeful responses" (Kranowitz, 2006a, p.3). When sensory processing difficulties exist, students may struggle with responding appropriately to sensory input, resulting in trouble with behavior, attention, or emotional regulation, for example (Miller, 2014). Movement, social relatedness, and learning may also be influenced (Kranowitz, 2006b). Clearly, the use of sensory strategies must be included in our repertoire if we want to keep our students regulated and available for learning in the classroom.

When considering sensory strategies for our students, we always consult with our occupational therapist to determine which one(s) might be appropriate given the student's sensory profile.

Some of the sensory strategies we use most frequently include:

- fidgets
- deep pressure: on arms/legs, squeezes, foam roller, "sandwich" in large mat
- weighted vest/lap pad
- heavy work
- walking, running, jumping
- swinging, wagon ride
- roll over exercise ball/upside down
- brushing, lotion
- bouncing on lap/exercise ball
- gum chewing/crunchy foods
- headphones
- covers on fluorescent lights
- seating: crate/tub, cube chair, wiggle cushion, t-stool.

For more sensory strategies and activities, consult *The Out-of-Sync Child Has Fun* (Kranowitz, 2006a) and *Self-Regulation Interventions and Strategies* (Garland, 2014).

SHOW AND TELL

CHAPTER 3

MODELING

Modeling is the demonstration of a behavior that can be reproduced by the observer (Corbett and Abdullah, 2005). It is based on Bandura's Social Learning Theory (1977), which proposes that human behavior is learned mainly by observing and imitating others. Modeling of behaviors can be presented live or via video recording, and the model can be an adult or a peer.

IN-VIVO MODELING

In-vivo modeling, in which a behavior is modeled by a live person, is one of the most effective ways to show a student with autism what to do in a given situation. It enhances predictability and helps him formulate his own plan for how to follow through. A student who is neurotypical will naturally look to other people to guide his own behavior. When he is in an unfamiliar situation and doesn't know how to behave or what to expect, he watches what other people are doing. This simple act of observing others increases his comfort level, keeps him calm, and helps him to know what to do when it is his turn. Because the student on the spectrum tends to be object-oriented, observing people is not natural for him (Rydell, 2012). He will often focus on an object or his own internal state, thus failing to observe what others are doing. He is subsequently at a loss as to what to do, causing anxiety and increasing the likelihood that dysregulation will occur.

In our practice, we model consistently and often. When we decide to use this strategy, we have two choices: model the behavior ourselves, or point out others who are modeling the behavior. As the student with autism has difficulty with saliency, or "determining the most important information in a given situation" (Williams and Minshew, 2010), we will most likely need to call his attention to what is being modeled. When demonstrating the desired behavior ourselves, we do this by making a noise (e.g. throat-clear, snap, foot-tap), using a subtle gesture, or by positioning ourselves near what we want the student to notice (Rydell, 2012). We avoid calling the student's name or giving a verbal cue because we want him to learn to watch other people naturally without becoming dependent on prompts from others to do so. By making a noise or moving into the student's line of vision, we are guiding him to look toward the salient information and increasing his independence in thinking through what he needs to do next (Rydell, 2012). If another adult is available, it is helpful to have that person call the student's attention by pointing and looking at the person modeling the behavior. For example, if one of us is modeling how to roll the dice properly during a board game, we might clear our throat and move the dice briefly into the student's line of vision. Then, with the student watching, we would model shaking the dice and dropping it onto the game board.

The inclusive classroom setting lends itself beautifully to using peer models. We often simply call the student's attention to a peer who is modeling the appropriate behavior. For example, if the student is standing at circle time and all the other kids are sitting, we might point to his peers and say, "All the kids are sitting," and then wait to give the student time to process the information. Alternatively, if we can get the student's attention with a silent point to his peers, we will just do that. These options are vastly different from giving the directive to "Sit down." We are teaching the student to observe other people and adjust his own behavior accordingly, rather than learning to wait for a prompt. We are moving him away from an object-oriented learning style and teaching him to learn from other people (Rydell, 2012).

VIDEO MODELING

Video modeling is another way to show a student with autism that he can watch other people to know what to do. This strategy enables the student to learn from a model without the added social demands of a face-to-face interaction (Corbett and Abdullah, 2005). Additionally, it can help with saliency, as the student's attention is concentrated on the pertinent information on the screen (Charlop-Christy, Le, and Freeman, 2000). That said, we consistently strive to involve the student with autism in the world of people. When using video modeling, we keep the video short and specific to the goal, and move the student along to watching in vivo models as quickly as possible.

For example, we used video modeling for a student in our classroom who was unable to complete the clean-up routine independently at the end of snack time. This student could be very distractible, especially in the classroom situation. We first tried pointing out a peer who was modeling the behavior, but he was unable to focus on the relevant information, even after many attempts. We decided to try video modeling. We made a video of a peer putting his cup in his lunchbox, throwing away his napkin, putting his lunchbox in his backpack, and then choosing a book for quiet reading. We then showed this short video to the student right after he finished eating, step by step at first, which enabled him to complete the routine successfully without multiple prompts. Once he could complete the clean-up routine successfully, we faded the video modeling.

Modeling, both live and via video, is an excellent strategy to use to help students on the autism spectrum stay regulated and learn to watch other people to gain information to guide their own behavior. This kind of observation is an essential life skill that does not come naturally to them. Showing the student what others are doing, and teaching him that he can watch people to know what to do, will greatly increase his ability to stay regulated and available for learning and engagement.

■ EXAMPLES

- You are working 1:1 with the student with autism and modeling how to build a block tower. He is starting to whine and look around the room. You tap the blocks together and move yourself into the student's line of vision, and then quickly build the tower once you've got his attention.

- It is circle time and the teacher is reading a book to the class. The student with autism is looking behind him at the classroom computer. You silently get down to his level and point and look toward the teacher from behind him, while using your arm to block his view of the computer. You may say, "Your friends are looking at Miss Lori."

- You are modeling an activity for the class that has several steps. Each student will be expected to take a turn and complete the same steps (e.g. jump on four circles, roll a ball through a tunnel, drop the ball in a bucket). While you are modeling, the student with autism is attending to something else in the room. You clear your throat and/or tap the ball until the student's attention returns to you. If that is unsuccessful, a colleague may point to you from behind the student to provide an additional cue. Once the student is attending to you, you continue the sequence. Tip: provide the student with autism with as many models as possible before he is expected to imitate the behavior, by having all the other peers go before him.

- The class is doing an activity where each student is expected to come up and take a turn (see above). A classmate is taking her turn, but the student with autism is looking at a different peer. You point to the student he should be watching and say, "I'm watching Emma."

- The student with autism continually begins talking to adults in the room without first gaining their attention. On many occasions, you have tried modeling how to gain a person's attention, but he is still not doing it. You create a short video on the iPad of a peer tapping a teacher's arm and saying her name to gain her attention. You show the video to the student on multiple occasions, while prompting him to practice the skill immediately afterward.

MODELING

Use this strategy throughout the day.

Benefits

- ✓ The student learns to observe others to guide his own behavior
- ✓ Reduces anxiety and dysregulation

Tips

In-vivo

- ✓ Call the student's attention to yourself:
  - Throat-clear, snap, foot-tap, tap object
  - Get in the student's line of vision
  - Comment about what you are doing
- ✓ Call the student's attention to others:
  - Silent point with eye gaze
  - Point and comment on what the model is doing

Video

- ✓ Short and specific to the goal
- ✓ Fade as quickly as possible

CHAPTER 4

SHOW HOW MANY/ SHOW HOW LONG

As educators, we need to require our students to complete tasks that they may prefer not to do. This is especially true with children on the autism spectrum. The rigid thinking patterns and inflexible attachment to routines that are hallmarks of autism (American Psychiatric Association, 2013) can manifest as a strict adherence to one's own agenda. Our task is very likely not on that student's predetermined agenda! So, from the very beginning, we may be interfering with what that student feels compelled to do (Rydell, n.d.). Additionally, our activity may be challenging for the student because of motor planning difficulties, communication challenges, or sensory integration differences, to name a few. If this difficult or non-preferred task is then presented to the child with no indication of how long he will be required to stay focused and participate, dysregulation may quickly ensue.

Think about your own mindset when embarking on a task that you are reluctant to complete (exercise comes to mind!). Having an idea of how many sit-ups you need to complete, or how long you must run, can help you to focus on the task, stay calm, and push through to completion.

Now think about the student with autism. Not only is he frequently asked to complete non-preferred tasks with no discernable endpoint, he also lacks the self-regulatory skills that you have as a neurotypical adult. As educators, we can easily help our student to see the endpoint by indicating "how many" he is expected to complete or "how long" he needs to participate before he is done (Mesibov *et al.*, 2004), helping him stay regulated and available for learning.

The literature supports the learning benefit of providing this type of structure for students on the autism spectrum. For example, the philosophy behind the Treatment and Education of Autistic and related Communication handicapped Children (TEACCH) methodology emphasizes the need to be precise when conveying expectations and instructions to students with autism (Ball, 2008). Specifically, during their discussion of "Work/Activity Systems," Mesibov *et al.* (2004) stipulate that it should be immediately and visually evident to the student "how much work" a given task requires or "how long" the activity will last (p.43-44). We have found that our students frequently need this kind of structure provided throughout the school day, during many different types of activities. Each individual task may need to be broken down and structured. One way we can do that is by providing the student with information about how many he needs to complete, or how long he is expected to participate, before he is finished.

We must provide this information in a way that is accessible to the student. Note the use of the word "show" embedded in the title of this strategy. When we use this strategy, we take advantage of the use of visuals to help the student fully comprehend the concept. In addition to aiding comprehension, providing visuals to show how many or how long helps the student hold the concept in his mind while he is completing the task. The sand timer sitting on the shelf, or the three puzzle pieces lying on the table, help the student to remember that there is a point of completion. This goes a long way toward helping him stay regulated and engaged and increases the chance that he will be able to finish the activity.

SHOW HOW MANY

Showing the student how many turns he must take, or how many turns remain, is a very effective strategy for keeping him calm and engaged. Any set of objects can be used to make the concept of "how many" come alive for a student. For example, when completing a puzzle with a student who is becoming dysregulated, we might point to the puzzle pieces and say, "Two more pieces, then all done." Making the turns as visually salient as possible will help the student quickly grasp the concept. This can be done by placing each object that is part of the activity inside a plastic ring or on a rubber shape. As each turn is completed, the student or adult can put the ring on a cone or put the shape in a bin. For students who have more language and cognitive ability, "how many" can be shown by drawing circles on a paper that he can cross out or fill in with a dot marker.

When using this strategy, we prefer to leave the number of items until "all done" flexible. That is, we choose how many items need to be completed based on the student's past performance and regulation in that moment. Sometimes, it might be reasonable for a student to complete a ten-piece puzzle; other times, he may only be able to do three. We must be free to adjust these expectations, using our expertise to determine what is appropriate and achievable. We constantly strive to find the balance between keeping the student regulated and pushing him just enough to move him along to the next level.

This strategy can be used proactively, at the outset of an activity, to let the student know how many turns will be expected. It can also be used during an activity that is in progress, should the student begin to become dysregulated. For example, perhaps we have begun doing a shape-sorting activity with a student. He is normally amenable to this activity and can complete the task of putting 12 shapes into the container. However, after three shapes, he begins to whine and attempt to leave. Since there are still nine shapes left, the expectation is likely too high right now. We might quickly and quietly slide six shapes out of the way and then get the student's attention and point to the three remaining shapes saying, "Three more, then all done." The task is now achievable for the student, and we can provide the support he needs to push through to completion.

SHOW HOW LONG

Showing the student how long he must stick with an activity is another way of helping him stay regulated. As time is a very abstract concept, we must make it especially visually salient for the child. It helps to make time increments small (one or two minutes), especially when first introducing this strategy. The passing of time can be shown using a sand timer (especially a large one), an iPad timer, or a Time Timer®. The timer should be set where the student can see but not touch it. If the timer becomes too distracting, we may remove it from view but continue to show it to the student periodically.

This strategy is also very useful when a student must give up a preferred item. For example, if the student is playing with a preferred puzzle and is refusing to give a peer a turn, we might say "One more minute, then give to Alex," and set the one-minute timer. Or, if the student has the capacity to make a choice, we might say, "Give the puzzle to Alex now or in one minute?" The student may still become dysregulated when it is time to give up the puzzle, but the warning and the timer will give him the chance to stay regulated and process the upcoming change, as well as the opportunity to begin to learn turn-taking.

Finally, this strategy can also be used to prepare the student for a transition, giving him time to make the cognitive shift from one task to another. For example, near the end of center time, we often give the warning, "Two more minutes, then circle time." An added visual, such as a two-minute timer and/or a picture icon of circle time, can help the student hold this upcoming transition in his mind and decrease dysregulation.

EXAMPLES
Show How Many

- You sit down with your student to draw a picture together as part of a language task. You want to draw a picture of you and the child playing with blocks, and use it to start a conversation about what you did. Your student is very wriggly and not able to attend to drawing the picture. You draw three circles on a separate piece of paper and say, "We need to draw three things: you, me, and the block tower." After each element is drawn, the child gets to cross out that circle.

- It is snack time and your student wants to leave the table after eating only one cracker. You want him to stay longer, giving him the chance to engage with you and his peers. You say, "Three more crackers, then all done," setting out three crackers in front of him. You then attempt to engage him, prolonging his time at the table.

- Your student is whining at circle time when the others are singing songs. It becomes clear that he wants circle time to end, so snack time can begin. You say, "One more song, then snack time."

Show How Long

- It is free-choice time and your student has chosen to go to the dramatic play center. However, as soon as he gets to dramatic play, he wants to leave and go to blocks. He has a habit of wandering from activity to activity, so one of his goals is to stay long enough at each location to engage with the materials and other students. You tell him, "Two minutes at dramatic play, then blocks," and set a visual timer where he can see it. You then provide him with a prompt to distract him and get him involved in the activity such as, "I'm hungry; I need some cake."

- Your student is in the block area and is whining because another student is playing with his favorite blue car. He is trying to grab the car from the peer. You stop him and say to the peer. "You've had the blue car for a while. Two minutes, then Jack's turn." You set a timer for two minutes and show Jack, saying, "Two minutes, then your turn," and then stay close to monitor the situation and engage Jack until it is his turn.

- Your student comes into class holding a favorite toy and does not want to relinquish it. It will be distracting for him to continue to hold it in his hand. You get out an "all done" container and say, "One more minute, then toy in." You set the one-minute timer where the child can see it. When one minute is over, you hold the container out so he can put the toy in. Give him ample opportunity to put it in on his own by waiting. Then, if needed, help him by using the least intrusive level of prompting that is necessary.

SHOW HOW MANY/SHOW HOW LONG

Benefits

- ✓ Provides structure and clarifies expectations
- ✓ Incorporates visuals
- ✓ Reduces anxiety and increases regulation

Tips

Show How Many

- ✓ Make "how many" visually apparent:
  - Gestures: point to and count each item
  - Emphasize with rubber shapes/plastic rings
- ✓ Keep "how many" flexible:
  - Use your judgment and experience
  - Modify as needed during the activity

Show How Long

- ✓ Use a visually accessible timer:
  - Sand timer (the bigger the better)
  - iPad timer; Time Timer®
- ✓ Stick to a short amount of time (one to two minutes)

CHAPTER 5

VERBALIZE A RULE

Verbalizing a rule can give the student with autism behavior-specific language to support self-regulation. This strategy can work well with students who are especially rule-bound. Being rule-bound is related to the ritualistic behavior that is one of the primary symptoms of autism (American Psychiatric Association, 2013). Of course, rigid thinking patterns can cause problems for the students with autism, as they may easily become "stuck" on events unfolding in a very particular way. However, as educators, we can capitalize on this tendency to be rule-bound to achieve positive outcomes for our students. Stating a rule can provide structure, clarify expectations, and help the student stay calm and regulated. Since this is a language-based strategy, it is only appropriate for use with students who have the language ability to support it. It is also only appropriate for students who have the cognitive ability to begin to regulate their own behavior.

As always, we provide positive behavior support when using this strategy. We state what we want the student to do, rather than what we don't want him to do. For example, if the student is running through the classroom, we could state, "The rule is: we walk in the classroom." We would never say, "The rule is: no running in the classroom." One reason is that, given language processing and/or attentional difficulties, the student may only hear the latter part of the statement, "running in the classroom," and interpret that as his imperative. More importantly, we want to model language that helps the student develop internal commentary of what he *should* do. This will help him make sense of the expectations so that he can have success and feel good about himself.

An alternative way of stating the rule is to present it as a script for the student (e.g. "I can walk to messy table"). Scripting, which is different than echolalic scripting in which a student repeats verbatim chunks of speech they have heard, is a recognised evidence-based practice for autism (National Professional Development Center on Autism Spectrum Disorder, n.d.). It was originally considered as a type of Social Narrative, but recently became recognized as a separate intervention (Griffin and AFIRM Team, 2017). Scripting includes only the content of what the student should say or do, without identifying the impact of the action on others, as a Social Narrative would do (Griffin and AFIRM Team, 2017). We believe that this simplification renders Scripting a more accessible strategy for the developmental level of our preschool students with autism. Much of the literature discusses Scripting as a tool to teach students with autism social interaction skills. We have found that it is also effective when used as a strategy to help students stay regulated. When we use this strategy with preschoolers, we keep the script short and simple and encourage the student to repeat the phrase to aid comprehension.

Once the rule is stated or the script is repeated, it is important to make sure the student follows through. For example, after the student repeats, "I can walk to the sink," we go right alongside him at first. If he begins to run/hop we stop him and say, "Walk." We then back him up to where he started to run and model the script again. We repeat this until the student can successfully walk from one location to another. Even when the student can reliably walk to the sink on his own, we continue to have an adult available at the sink to receive him and facilitate continued regulation as he begins the hand-washing routine. Finally, we strive to fade scripts as early as possible and are careful not to overuse them.

■ EXAMPLES

- Your student tends to become dysregulated when walking in the hallway. He will often suddenly reach out and rip posters/art projects off the wall as he walks by.
  - Rule: You say, "Hands in pockets in the hallway," or "The rule is: squeeze hands together in the hall."
  - Script: As you begin to walk in the hall, you model, "I can squeeze my hands," and encourage the child to repeat the phrase as he squeezes his hands.
- Your student has difficulty walking from one location to another in the classroom. He tends to run or hop, without regard for who/what he might run into.
  - Rule: You say, "We walk in the classroom."
  - Script: Before the student begins to transition to the easel, you model, "I can walk to easel," and wait for the student to repeat it.
- Your student wants to hug everyone in the class, without regard for whether they want to be hugged. The hugs can sometimes be a little too enthusiastic.
  - Rule: You say, "The rule is: high-fives at school" and then model this behavior for the student.
  - Script: "I can high-five my friends."
- Your student is working at the easel and wants to put the paintbrush in his mouth instead of the cup of water.
  - Rule: You say, "The brush goes in the cup."
  - Script: "My brush goes in the cup," or "Brush in cup."

- Your student is washing his hands and wants to pull the lever on the paper towel dispenser over and over, dispensing too much paper towel.
  - Rule: You say, "The rule is: one, two, three, stop."
  - Script: "I can pull three times," or "One, two, three, stop."

VERBALIZE A RULE

Benefits

- ✓ Provides structure and clarifies the expectation
- ✓ Helps students begin to regulate their own behavior

Tips

- ✓ An adult must be available to help the student follow through at first

Rule

- ✓ State what you *do* want the student to do, e.g. "The rule is: [pause] Walk in the classroom"
- ✓ Use simple, direct language

Script

- ✓ State the rule as a script that the student can repeat for himself, e.g. "I can walk to the sink"
- ✓ Wait and give the student time to repeat the script before proceeding
- ✓ Avoid overusing scripts and fade at the earliest opportunity

MOVING ON

CHAPTER 6

FIRST/THEN

The First/Then strategy is one of the most frequently utilized strategies for students with autism. Many practitioners report familiarity with this strategy, as well as successful use with all students. We use this strategy so often with our students that we considered including it as one of our Three Guidelines. As we mentioned in Chapter 1, when a student is beginning to become dysregulated, the first thing we do is think through our Three Guidelines to determine if we have adequately employed them in the current situation. We consider whether we have provided sufficient processing time, used simple and direct language, and utilized appropriate visuals. Often, the very next thing we do is give the student a First/Then.

The basis of the First/Then is the well-known positive reinforcement strategy, the Premack principle. This principle of operant conditioning, identified by psychologist David Premack (1965), simply means that high-probability behaviors can be used to reinforce low-probability behaviors. Essentially, the promise of a preferred activity increases the student's motivation to complete a less preferred or more challenging task (Wiseman and Hunt, 2008).

Additionally, the First/Then strategy reflects one of the basic tenets of structured teaching. Clearly stating the non-preferred or required activity, and then the preferred activity, provides structure and clarifies the expectation. It immediately and directly makes it evident to the student what must be done now and what will happen next. Providing this structure reduces anxiety for the student with ASD by increasing certainty and predictability (Mesibov *et al.*, 2004). Thus, the student is much more likely to stay regulated and available for learning.

Finally, this strategy naturally makes use of simple, direct language, which aids comprehension. One of the most important points to remember when using this strategy is to *stop talking* once you have communicated the First/Then. For example, if the child runs straight to the snack table, we might say, "First wash hands, then snack." The only other talking we would do at this point might be to simply restate the First/Then. We would not give the student additional language to process by saying things like, "Come on. It's time to eat. We need to wash our hands. Let's go into the bathroom…" and so on.

When a verbal First/Then is not successful, we quickly add a visual. Because we use this strategy so often, we have First/Then materials placed in pockets that are strategically hung throughout our room. That way, when a student is becoming dysregulated, we don't have to leave his side or call to another staff member to bring us a visual. Each pocket (made with a colorful file folder) contains several simple First/Then boards, as well as boards containing commonly used classroom icons. For example, we include icons representing every area in the classroom (blocks, sink, blue table, etc.). We also include icons representing every activity we do during the day (circle time, wash hands, etc.), as well as icons of sand timers indicating "one more minute" and "two more minutes." This way, we can quickly grab two icons and a board to create a visual to support almost any situation we might come across. Once we have presented the visual to the child, we put it (or hold it) where he can see it, stay near him, and give him time to process the direction.

Figure 6.1 First/Then visual

Once we have communicated a First/Then to a student, verbally and/or visually, we intentionally do not engage with the student beyond providing the necessary cues to support the original message. We do not want to reinforce the refusal behavior or confuse him with further information to process. We would avoid eye contact and perhaps turn our body slightly away from him, while staying nearby to lend support and send the message that we are ready once he is. This is less confrontational, and gives the student the space to process the expectation and make the decision to proceed. Once the child starts to calm down and move on, we quickly reconnect with him (without a lot of talking!) and lend support where needed.

EXAMPLES

- The student does not want to do his pre-writing shapes. You say, "First shapes, then snack."

- The student has not helped clean up in the block center at the end of center time. He is becoming dysregulated because he is anxious about getting to circle time (the next activity) ahead of the other students. You say, "First clean up [pause]. Three blocks, then circle." Adding in the pause enables you to use specific language while still allowing the student time for processing, and to keep the direction simple.

- The student is refusing to put his coat on for outside time. You say, "First coat, then outside." You give him one repetition and ample processing time, but he is still not responding. You add a visual First/Then board with a picture of a coat and a picture of the playground.

- The student wants to switch activities as soon as he gets to blocks (the one he has chosen). One of his goals is to make a choice and follow through on it. You say, "First build *one* tower, then new center."

- You are doing a motivating activity at circle time. You are calling each student up for a turn. Your student is becoming anxious and starting to whine because he wants his turn. You choose another student to go before him and say, "First Jack's turn, then your turn." To make sure he understands, after a pause for processing, you can reiterate, "First Jack, then Mark [pause]. Wait [with gesture]."

FIRST/THEN

This is often the first strategy used after checking the Three Guidelines.

Benefits

✓ Provides structure and clarifies the expectation

✓ Decreases anxiety and dysregulation

Tips

Verbal

✓ Ensure that you have employed the Three Guidelines

✓ Give a verbal First/Then

- Stop talking once the First/Then has been stated

- Wait, while staying nearby but avoiding eye contact

- Reconnect and provide support as soon as the student is ready to move on

Visual

✓ Quickly add a visual if the student doesn't respond promptly

- Keep the visual in the student's view once presented

- Wait and give him time to process and respond

- **Post First/Then pockets around your classroom**

CHAPTER 7

OFFER A CHOICE

It is well documented in the literature that offering choices can increase regulation and reduce difficult behaviors in students with autism. In fact, Prizant *et al.* (2006) suggest that giving the student a choice empowers him by permitting him to apply some social control. In addition to empowering the student, giving a choice can distract him from his own agenda. The rigid thinking patterns of students with autism sometimes cause them to get stuck on doing (or not doing) something at a particular time, in a particular way (American Psychiatric Association, 2013). Giving a choice can momentarily divert the student's attention from that agenda so that he can be redirected. Offering a choice can be a very effective strategy for students who have the cognitive and communicative ability to make choices.

When giving a choice, we present only two options, both of which fit within our expectations. The student feels empowered, because he is choosing, while still working toward completing the activity we have presented. Presenting only two options sets the student up to have the best chance of processing what he needs to do, making the choice, and moving on. Sticking to the two choices we originally presented also helps us avoid getting pulled into a negotiation. Even if the "third choice" the student comes up with seems reasonable, he must choose from the original two options.

Within any activity, there are multiple ways to give the student a choice. As educators, we use what we know about each student to offer the choice that will be the most effective for him. Choices can be given regarding an object or activity, positioning, timing, location, or level of assistance. For example, when the student is refusing to write, there are many possible choices that can be given to help him stay regulated and move on. We might give him a choice regarding the object (e.g. "Do you want the red crayon or green crayon?"), positioning (e.g. "Do you want to write standing up or sitting down?"), timing (e.g. "Do you want to start now or in one minute?"), location (e.g. "Do you want to write at the blue table or yellow table?"), or level of assistance (e.g. "Do you want to write by yourself or with help?").

Timing choices are especially helpful when the student must give up a preferred object or activity. For example, suppose it is free-choice time and the student has been at the water table for a long time. It is time for him to move to a new area, but he begins to protest. We might say, "Time for a new activity. Choose now or in one minute?" At this point, more often than we expect, the student will just make a choice and move on. Most of the time, he will choose to stay for one more minute. At that point, we set a timer for one minute and gather visuals for two centers that we know he also likes. As soon as the one minute is done, we call the student's attention to the timer and say, "Water table is all done. Choose a new activity," while presenting the two options.

Timing choices are also helpful when the student must wait for a turn to play with a preferred object or activity. For example, the student wants to play at the art table, but it is full. We would count the peers and show him that the table is full. We might then select a peer who has been at that activity for a while, letting him know that he has two more minutes at art and setting a timer as a visual reminder of the upcoming transition for both students. We would then engage the student with autism in an alternative activity until the two minutes were up.

Level of assistance choices can be especially helpful for a student who is reluctant to initiate a task. It may be that he is having difficulty with initiation or that sequencing of the task and/or motor planning are difficult. Giving the student the option to begin with assistance can get him over the hump and moving along. When giving assistance in this way, we fade our support quickly—as soon as we see the student begin to proceed on his own.

As previously mentioned, giving the student a choice not only empowers him, it may also distract him from his agenda. For example, it is departure time and all the students are putting on their coats and backpacks. The student with autism is refusing to put his coat on, and we know he has the skills to do this independently. Rather than getting into a power struggle, we might opt to distract him by giving a choice, "Right sleeve first or left?" When he chooses, we quickly slip that sleeve on and then prompt him to "Keep going." This is often enough to momentarily distract him so that he can complete the task.

■ EXAMPLES
Object/Activity

- The student is squirmy and dysregulated at circle time. He is usually better able to sit and focus when he is holding a fidget. You hold out two fidgets and say, "Jack, clicker or squishy ball?"

- The student is becoming dysregulated because he wants to go to the block area and it is full. You say, "Blocks later.

Water table or easel?" (making sure that these are both centers that the child also likes).

Positioning

- The student frequently becomes dysregulated while walking in the hallway, causing him to rip things off the wall impulsively. You say, "Daniel, hands in pockets or squeeze together. Which one?" Once the child is familiar with this choice, and if it will be a consistently used strategy, you can simplify by just saying, "Daniel, hands in pockets or squeeze?" with accompanying gestures.

- It is story time and the student with autism is lying on his back at circle. The other students are lying on their tummies. You say, "Story time. Tummy or sit criss-cross?"

Timing

- The student is becoming dysregulated because a peer wants the car he is playing with. You say, "Joey needs a turn. Give to him now or in one minute. Which one?" You follow up by setting up a one-minute visual timer.

- You have changed the daily schedule around due to unforeseen circumstances. It is time to go outside, but the student is refusing to line up because he is stuck on the fact that it should be snack time. You say, "Time to go outside. Line up now or in one minute?"

Location

- You need to work individually with the child on a puzzle, but he wants to do something else. You say, "Time for the puzzle. On the table or on the floor?"

- The student is refusing to wash his hands at snack time. You say, "Wash hands. Kitchen sink or bathroom sink?"

Assistance

- The student has become dysregulated at circle time because another student did not choose the song he wanted. He is lying down in the middle of circle and crying. You say, "Time to sit on your carpet square. Need help or by yourself?"

- The class is doing a group water-balloon activity. It is your student's turn to toss his balloon, but he is worried about getting wet and is beginning to refuse and whine. You say, "Everyone is tossing a balloon. Do it by yourself or with help?"

OFFER A CHOICE

Benefits

- ✓ Gives the student some power
- ✓ May distract the student from his agenda

Tips

- ✓ Give two options:
  - Both must fit within your agenda
  - Avoid negotiation by sticking to the two options
- ✓ Multiple ways to give a choice:
  - Object or activity (Red crayon or green crayon?)
  - Positioning (On your tummy or criss-cross?)
  - Timing (Now or in one minute?)
  - Location (At the table or on the floor?)
  - Level of assistance (By yourself or with help?)

CHAPTER 8

I START/YOU FINISH

It is not unusual for a student with autism to experience difficulty when beginning a new task. Perhaps the work is challenging for the student or simply not their preferred activity. It may be that the activity is not on the student's agenda right now—he had a completely different plan in mind. Difficulty with organizing and sequencing (Mesibov *et al.*, 2004) the steps to completion may also cause the student to struggle with initiating a new task. Additionally, shifting his attention and transitioning from a previous activity to the current one may be troublesome. For any one of these reasons, or a combination of them, beginning a new activity may be problematic for the student with autism. Even when the work is well within his abilities, he may experience significant hurdles in getting started. Sometimes, just a little boost to get beyond the initiation of the endeavor is all the student needs to stay regulated and on task.

When using this strategy, we begin the task and the student finishes it. If needed, we might scaffold the activity and complete all the steps except the last one and work backwards over time (Rydell, 2012). For example, if the student is refusing to write his name (and we know he has the skills), we might begin by writing all the letters except the last one. The student finishes the exercise by completing the last letter. This may make the task seem less overwhelming, allowing the student to stay regulated and participate in an activity that is not on his agenda.

Similar concepts include doing the task together or taking turns. For the above example, doing the task together might entail doing the first couple of letters hand-over-hand and then backing off and letting the student complete the other letters on his own. If opting for taking turns, we might say, "My turn," and write the first letter and then hand the crayon to the student and say, "Your turn." Any of these strategies can be successful in getting the student over his difficulty in initiating the activity. We use our knowledge of each individual student to determine which one is likely to have the most success in the given situation.

When using this strategy, we must remain especially mindful that students with autism are at risk of becoming prompt-dependent. We do not want our students to learn to wait for a prompt or a cue to begin a task. For that reason, we first *wait* and provide plenty of time to determine if the student will begin the activity on his own. If not, we provide the minimal amount of prompting necessary to get the student going. We are also careful to vary the type of prompt provided so that we are not providing the same prompt in the same situation each time. For example, we might use a light touch to the elbow (tactile prompt) one time and a contact point to the task (gestural prompt) the next. Finally, we ensure that we are careful to fade prompts as quickly as possible.

▓ EXAMPLES

- The student is refusing to complete a puzzle. You say, "I'll start," put in a few pieces and then hand one to the student.

- The student is melting down when asked to pass out the snacks to his peers. You say, "Let's do it together," and begin the process, including the student, but shifting to the student doing it independently as quickly as possible.

- The student has watched several students take their turn in a game. However, when it is his turn, he doesn't seem to know what to do and is starting to get up. You say, "My turn, then your turn," and then quickly demonstrate the desired action while you've got the student's attention.

- The student is standing and staring at the coat rack when it is time to complete the arrival routine (e.g. hang up backpack, take off coat and hang up, get out snack). You do the first step (hang up backpack), begin to unzip the coat hand-over-hand with the student, and then let go and say, "Keep going."

- The student is crying and saying, "I can't," when asked to participate in a simple art activity. You say, "I'll start," and glue the first couple of pieces. You then hand the glue to the student and say, "Keep going," or "Three more, you do it."

I START/YOU FINISH

Use this strategy to help a student initiate a task

- ✓ The adult begins the task and the student completes it
  - • You can do all but one step together and then work backward
- ✓ The adult and student do it together
  - • You can begin with a physical prompt and then quickly fade
- ✓ The adult and student take turns

HELPING HANDS

CHAPTER 9

SIMPLE TASKS

It is well documented in the literature that students with autism have difficulty organizing and sequencing information. Simultaneously attending to both the present circumstance, as well as the intended outcome, can be particularly challenging for our students (Mesibov *et al.*, 2004). Simple tasks provide external organization and a defined endpoint, freeing the student to concentrate solely on the immediate task. The visual organization of simple tasks also increases their predictability, reducing anxiety and promoting regulation (Mesibov *et al.*, 2004). Additionally, simple tasks incorporate repetitive motor movements, which can ameliorate the "challenges to bodily rhythm and timing" that our students may experience (Amos, 2013, p.2). Thus, simple tasks can be regulating both cognitively and motorically.

When choosing a simple task, several parameters must be considered. Most importantly, as previously mentioned, the student must be familiar with the task and able to complete it independently. This is not a time to teach new skills. We must ensure that the student has not only the cognitive skills to understand the task, but also the motor skills to do so. Since we work with young children, we must consider whether the objects present a choking hazard. Finally, if the objects provided are overly interesting to the student, causing him to engage in self-stimulatory behavior, that activity may need to be eliminated. For example, we had one student who was only interested in putting the shape sorter pieces on the tips of his fingers and waving them in front of his eyes. Using the toy functionally required adult intervention. We replaced the shape sorter with a simple task that did not have pieces he could balance on the ends of his fingers.

Early developmental toys that have a clear beginning and end are one type of simple task that we use. Toys that work well for our preschool students include shape sorters, simple puzzles, large stringing beads, and ring stackers. These activities may require students to have certain cognitive skills, such as matching, sorting (e.g. the shape sorter) and beginning sequencing (e.g. the ring stacker). Motor skills must also be considered, as the student must be able to manipulate the objects easily. Remember, to serve as a regulating task, the student must be able to complete the task independently. If he is unable to do that, the activity must be taught when the student is regulated and available for learning.

For students who are at an earlier developmental level, we may need to start with a simple put-in task. This sort of task requires the student to focus on only one element: picking up an object and putting it in a container. Put-in tasks are the beginning level of independent work (Reeve and Kabot, 2012). Simply picking up a block and dropping it in a bucket would be the most rudimentary level of put-in. We have put-ins assembled and placed in bins throughout the classroom so they are ready to be used at a moment's notice.

We create put-ins for our classroom out of plastic food containers for cream cheese, butter, yogurt, gum, or any other small container that has a lid. One of our favorites is a clear parmesan cheese container, which allows the student to see the objects as they drop them in. The container must have a lid with some sort of opening, or a slit can be cut in the top of the lid. The size of the put-in container depends on the student's level of bilateral coordination. Larger containers will require problem-solving skills to figure out how to stabilize the container.

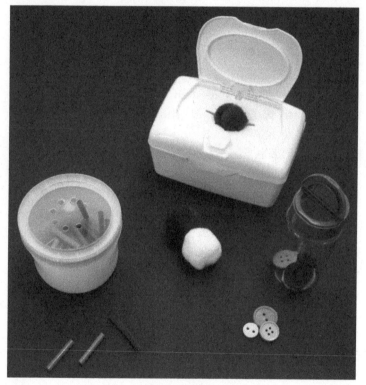

Figure 9.1 Put-ins

Objects for the put-in can be buttons, cut up sponges, beads, pom-poms (sparkly ones are great!) or any object that the student can independently manipulate. The put-in may be a random set of small objects in a container or it could be customized to match the activity the rest of the class is doing. For instance, during story time, the put-in may be small, laminated pictures taken directly from the book being read, which are slipped through a small slit in the lid of the put-in. Another option is to customize the put-in to match specific student interests. As mentioned earlier, we are always careful when we do this to find a balance in a put-in between it being enticing but not becoming the sole focus of the student's attention. Finally, it can be beneficial to increase the level of challenge of the put-in to prevent boredom and match the student's abilities. For example, a put-in can be upgraded to a sorting task by making two slits in the lid and using permanent marker to color code them. The student would then be given objects of those two colors to sort as he puts them in the container. *Tasks Galore* (Eckenrode, Fennell, and Hearsey, 2013) contains a multitude of ideas for creating put-ins and other tasks.

We use simple tasks preventatively, as well as in response to an escalation in dysregulation. Used preventatively, simple tasks can help a student stay regulated during transitions, as well as when waiting is required. Simple tasks can also be helpful at times when doing something with his hands will help a student stay put, giving him the opportunity to engage with the class activity. The best example of this is put-ins at circle time. When one of our students has difficulty sitting at circle time, we may offer a put-in if this type of task is within his skill set. The put-in should be interesting enough to motivate the student to complete it, but not so preferred that he fixates on it and blocks everything else out. Initially, the student should glance up from the put-in to observe the teacher, and this behavior should increase over time. At circle time, we try to use put-ins that are quiet and not so large as to obscure the student's view or attract the attention of students sitting nearby. Some put-ins work best with a work surface. If our student sits in a cube chair, we can add a tray or put an upside-down cube chair in front of him. We had one student who sat on his carpet square with a tray. For some students, we initially need to give the put-in pieces one at a time to regulate speed and prevent self-stimulatory behavior with the objects. Later, we can put all the objects on the work surface or in the side pocket of the tray.

Some students respond well to being offered a simple task when dysregulated. This strategy will even help some to come down from a state of extreme dysregulation. To use this strategy, we might sit near the student and offer a simple task by setting it near him or perhaps calmly and quietly (no language!) playing with it ourselves for a bit and then handing it to or sliding it near the student once he notices it. If he refuses the task we have offered, or does not show interest in it, we try a different one. Once the child starts to engage with the materials, we stay near him but don't talk or attempt to engage him yet. He will need to interact only with the objects for a bit to help regulate himself. If he starts to include us with eye gaze and/or he seems to be returning to a state of equilibrium, we slowly start to interact with him and re-establish a connection.

There are some students who may be capable of, and benefit from, completing several simple tasks in a row. For these students, we set up work drawers in the style of work systems described in *The TEACCH Approach to Autism Spectrum Disorders* (Mesibov *et al.*, 2004). That is, we ensure that the system visually shows *what work* needs to be done, *how much* work needs to be done, *when* the student will be finished, and *what comes next* (Mesibov *et al.*, 2004). Detailed information about how to create work systems is available in *Building Independence: How to Create and Use Structured Work Systems* (Reeve and Kabot, 2012). The student always works from left to right (Mesibov *et al.*, 2004). He takes a drawer from the left, completes the task on the table in front of him, and then finishes by putting the drawer on the "all done" icon to his right. Our work drawer station is set up away from other distractions in the classroom. For some of our students, completing a series of work drawers at the beginning of the day can help them cope with this large transition and begin the day in a regulated state. We have also used work drawers for students who are consistently becoming dysregulated at a certain time of the day or during a specific activity. For example, one of our students regularly became dysregulated toward the end of free-choice time, throwing objects and swiping them to the floor. We initially responded with an increase in structure, by providing a visual schedule of activities for free-choice time. The behavior persisted, so we added more structure by including a work drawer session as the last item on his schedule. He would go to three different areas and then to the work drawers. Once he had completed his set of work drawers, the student would take his circle time icon and join his peers at circle. Not only did this provide the structure he needed to stay regulated through the end of free-choice time, but it also took him out of the chaos as the other students cleaned up and assembled for goodbye circle.

EXAMPLES

- Your student keeps trying to get up and leave at circle time. You think he has the cognitive ability and language skills to benefit from observing and/or participating in this activity. You have provided sensory supports for him, such as a weighted lap pad, deep pressure on his arms, and perhaps a fidget for him to hold. These do not seem to be enough to keep him regulated and engaged, so you offer a put-in in place of the fidget.

- Your student continually slides out of his chair onto the floor at snack time. Again, you have provided appropriate sensory supports, perhaps including headphones for excessive noise/chaos and a cube chair to provide additional support. Your student is still having difficulty staying seated. In addition to considering shortening the time he is expected to sit at the table (with the idea of lengthening it over time), you engage him with a simple inset puzzle (or a put-in) to keep him occupied and regulated between bites of snack.

- Your student is extremely dysregulated and is kicking, screaming, and rolling on the floor. In the past, he has found the ring stacker to be calming and organizing. You sit near him as he begins the process of calming down (he may still be very dysregulated) and start to play with the ring stacker quietly. At this point, you don't talk at all, and you don't try to engage your student in an interaction. You play silently until you see him start to glance toward you and the toy. At that point, you can either hold a ring toward the student (without eye contact) or set it on the floor near him. Once he starts to play with the rings, let him be. He will need to engage with the rings on his own for a while to organize and calm himself. When he is much calmer, and perhaps starts to glance toward you, you can make quiet, one-word comments/exclamations about what he is doing. Little by little, as he returns to a regulated state, you can fully engage with him and the toy as part of the process of reconnecting with him.

SIMPLE TASKS

Benefits

✓ Regulating due to visual organization, repetition, familiarity

Types

✓ Early developmental toys

✓ Put-ins

✓ Work drawers

Uses

✓ Preventatively to help a student stay regulated:

- During transitions
- When waiting
- To help him stay put and attend to group activity

✓ To help a student recover from dysregulation

Tips

✓ The student must be able to complete the task independently

✓ Avoid tasks that result in self-stimulatory behavior

✓ Gradually increase the time between tokens and the number of tokens needed

CHAPTER 10

INCENTIVE CHARTS

Incentive charts, which are a type of token system, are another visual strategy that we sometimes use with our students on the autism spectrum. There are several reasons that a system of external rewards may be especially effective with students with ASD. One reason is that some of these students may not be as intrinsically driven to learn as their peers (Prizant and Laurent, 2014). Another factor may be difficulty with theory of mind, or the ability to recognize that others have thoughts, desires and emotions that are different from their own (Baron-Cohen, 2001). This difficulty with perspective-taking (Winner, 2007) may diminish the motivation to adjust their behavior to the expectations of others. Finally, early learners on the autism spectrum, especially those with significant social learning challenges, may require reinforcement via external rewards, as they do not yet have the social perspective to appreciate the intrinsic value of positive social connection (Winner and Abildgaard, 2010; Winner and Crooke, 2013). For these reasons, a system of external rewards may be necessary to shape behavior in some instances.

Employing an incentive chart is a strategy that we consider after all other strategies have been attempted and after a functional behavior assessment has been completed to define the targeted behavior, as well as to identify the purpose of the behavior and the factors that sustain it (Kaiser and Rasminsky, 2012; Sam and AFIRM Team, 2015). An incentive chart can increase a student's level of self-awareness and help him begin to monitor his own behavior. However, this tool can also put our students at risk of developing an over-reliance on material, non-social rewards (Prizant and Laurent, 2014), and as such, reward charts/token systems need to be used judiciously. Accordingly, we do not use incentive charts across the day, nor with any longevity, and we limit their use to specific, well-defined behaviors. As soon as the specific desired behavior is learned, we fade the use of the incentive chart. For a student who has the cognitive and social ability to respond to social rewards, we work very hard to identify an alternative strategy to use in the first place.

Prizant and Laurent (2014) point out that token systems are quite complicated, requiring students to have certain skills and cognitive abilities to respond to them successfully. The student must have the symbolic capacity to understand that a token represents a preferred item or activity that he is working to earn (Prizant and Laurent, 2014). He must also be able to comprehend the behavioral expectation, as well as "demonstrate the self-regulatory ability necessary to delay gratification" (Prizant and Laurent, 2014, p.47). If the student does not have these skills, the token system will not have meaning for him. So, there is rather a narrow band of students who have the cognitive ability to comprehend a token system but are not yet responding to relationship-based rewards. This is another reason that we are very careful when considering using this strategy.

When we decide to implement an incentive chart, we have certain guidelines, or rules, that we follow. As was mentioned earlier, we always target a specific, well-defined behavior (e.g. sitting at circle without touching peers). We give tokens for the desired behavior and never remove tokens for undesired behavior (Prizant and Laurent, 2014). The goal is to reach the reward quickly and definitively. Taking tokens away is punitive and counterproductive to that purpose. When giving a token, we usually pair it with verbal affirmation of the desired behavior (e.g. "Your hands are in your lap!") said quickly and quietly to the student. On occasion, we've had to discontinue the verbalization when it completely distracted the student and those around him. Finally, we never require the student to "earn what is regulating and organizing" (Prizant and Laurent, 2014, p.48) for the activity at hand. For example, if a weighted lap pad helps a child stay regulated at circle time, then he would not be required to earn that as a reward if an incentive chart was also being used.

When creating an incentive chart, we ensure that it clearly shows the student what he is working for, as well as how many tokens he needs to accumulate to earn the reward. It is essential to collaborate with the student to incorporate his interests when creating the chart. One way to do this is to create tokens using pictures related to a preferred topic or area of interest (e.g. laminated train stickers). Another way to incorporate student preferences is to involve the student in choosing rewards. It is good to identify several rewards so the student can have a choice as to what he is working for each time. Since the students who can successfully use incentive charts must be at a certain level symbolically, we are typically able to use line drawings to represent the reward. However, there have been a few cases where the student needed to see the actual tangible reward (e.g. a toy car), in which case we put it in a clear box, which we Velcroed to the incentive chart.

One of our favorite types of reward is a short playtime with a preferred toy or activity. For example, when using an incentive chart at circle time, upon earning this reward the student would leave circle, sit at a table, play with a preferred toy for one minute (with a visual timer), and then return to circle. This can be disruptive for some, so it's very important to determine what will work best for each student. Other rewards might include going for a short walk or wagon ride, getting to do a special job or "be the teacher," a preferred gross motor activity, or a hand stamp. We try to move to a non-tangible, social reward as soon as possible.

To implement the incentive chart, we begin by presenting the agreed-upon rewards, let the student choose what he will be working for, and attach the icon to the chart. We make sure the student is aware of how many tokens are needed to earn the reward. Finally, we define the specific behavior for which tokens will be given. One example might be that the student is working on keeping his hands to himself at circle time, has chosen to play with a preferred toy as his reward, and needs to earn five tokens to earn the reward. We might say "hands in lap" and then point to the empty Velcro pieces on the chart as we count them, "One, two, three, four, five," and then point to the reward icon and say, "then car."

Figure 10.1 Incentive chart

When first using the chart, it is vital that the student makes the connection between the behavior and the reward. He needs to see quickly that the desired behavior earns a token and that the prescribed number of tokens earns him his chosen reward. To do this, the adult who is working with the student will need to give each token very rapidly—as soon as the desired behavior is witnessed. Additionally, the number of tokens needed to earn the reward will also need to be small—three or fewer. Gradually, the time between tokens is lengthened and the number of tokens needed to earn the reward is increased. It is important to stagger these adjustments, so that the student does not become confused or overwhelmed.

Our goal is to move the student through this process as rapidly as possible, reinforcing the desired behavior while drawing attention to more social rewards at the same time. We do this by pairing the agreed-upon, tangible reward with social rewards as soon as possible (Prizant and Laurent, 2014). We already mentioned quietly affirming the target behavior with each token, if it is not too distracting for the student (e.g. "Your hands are in your lap!"). Upon earning the reward, we would add a thumbs-up, high-five, and, most definitely, a smile and a head nod. Depending on the awareness level of the student, we might also give social praise to a nearby peer for the same behavior, so that our student with autism witnesses other students receiving and responding to social rewards (e.g. "Jack, your hands are in your lap!" with a pat on the back). Finally, once our students are ready, we add a "verbal explanation of others' thinking and feelings" as related to their behavior to help "pave the way for more finely tuned social understanding to develop" (Winner and Abildgaard, 2010, p.31).

As the time between tokens lengthens, and the number of tokens increases, the process of fading the incentive chart has begun. Another tactic we use to move this process along is to make the reward less interesting over time, when possible. For example, we might subtly alter the activities at the one-minute "play" time, or simply decrease the variety. The goal is for the student to find the activity that the group is doing (e.g. circle time) more captivating than the reward. We have even gotten to the point where we can give the student the choice of accepting the earned reward or staying with the class activity. Once the student values the class activity over the tangible reward, we know we can quickly fade the use of the chart.

Finally, when we have implemented an incentive chart and the student's behavior increases or simply does not change, we immediately reevaluate the process in which the chart is being used. We may need to give incentives more quickly, change the reward, or incorporate more student choice. It is also worth evaluating if giving concentrated attention to the behavior is making it worse. This is a great time to take another look at the functional behavior assessment (Kaiser and Rasminsky, 2012). Of course, it is important to reevaluate the use of all strategies constantly. Given the potential pitfalls of token systems, it is especially important to do so when an incentive chart has been implemented. As always, we must be ready to adjust our approach and shift strategies to respond to the complex nature of behavior and meet the needs of our students.

■ EXAMPLES

- Your student has difficulty waiting in line for a turn to wash his hands. He pushes himself directly to the sink every time. You have tried several other strategies, including using visuals to add structure and show him where to stand and how many students are ahead of him. You've also tried modeling by pointing out how peers are waiting for a turn, as well as verbalizing a rule. You've given each strategy ample time to work, but the student isn't responding to any of them reliably. You implement an incentive chart for this specific behavior to help the student learn exactly what he needs to do to wait successfully in line to wash his hands. Our classroom has large icons of different shoes taped to the floor to show each child where to stand in line. So, we might reinforce "Stand on green boots," and then label "Wait." Of course, we would also begin by requiring our student to wait behind only *one* other student, and then increase the number as his skills improve.

- Your student has started putting his hands in his mouth to play with his tongue at circle time, a behavior that has rapidly escalated. You have consulted with your occupational therapist to determine some appropriate sensory replacements, giving a choice between a couple of these where possible (e.g. gum or chewy toy). You've also tried giving the student a simple task, such as a put-in, to occupy his hands and distract him from the urge to put his hands in his mouth. You have added structure to the situation by showing how long the activity will last. The student is not responding to these strategies over time, so you implement an incentive chart to reinforce a behavior that will replace the undesired behavior (e.g. "hands on knees").

INCENTIVE CHARTS

Benefits

- ✓ Can help students begin to monitor their own behavior

Rules for use

- ✓ Use after other strategies have been tried
- ✓ Use only for a specific, well-defined behavior
- ✓ Give tokens for desired behavior, never take tokens away
- ✓ Pair with relationship-based, non-tangible rewards
- ✓ Fade use of the chart as soon as possible

Create chart

- ✓ Use student's interests when creating the chart
- ✓ Collaborate with the student/family on reward choices
- ✓ Show what the student is working for and how many tokens must be earned for reward

Teach

- ✓ Give tokens quickly at first
- ✓ Require three or fewer tokens to earn rewards initially
- ✓ Gradually increase time between tokens and the number of tokens needed

CHAPTER 11

VISUAL SCHEDULES

In Chapter 1, we touched on some of the benefits of visual support for students on the autism spectrum. Students with autism respond to visual support because it complements their learning style and aids comprehension. In addition, it is well documented that students on the autism spectrum struggle with sequencing and organizing activities, as well as with initiation. Specifically, MacDuff, Krantz, and McClannahan (1993) found that, even when a student with autism has learned how to complete the individual tasks in a sequence, he may need prompts to initiate each activity within that chain. For example, the student may have learned how to hang up his backpack, take off his coat, and get out his snack, but may still have difficulty chaining these actions together to complete the arrival routine at school. Thus, visual schedules complement the visual learning style of students with ASD, while also addressing a relative weakness in organizing and sequencing information.

The non-transient nature of the visual schedule allows the student to see clearly what is coming next and the time to process upcoming transitions. This predictability decreases anxiety, helping the student stay calm and regulated (Mesibov *et al.*, 2004). The visual schedule also promotes flexibility, as the student can see alterations to the schedule as icons are interchanged, removed, or added. The consistency of the schedule system itself helps the student stay calm and flexible as daily events shift and change. It is our responsibility as educators to build variation into our students' schedules, so that they can stay regulated through life's inevitable fluctuations.

Finally, visual schedules promote independence. By removing the adult from transitions, especially non-preferred transitions, the likelihood of protest and challenging behaviors is reduced (Mesibov *et al.*, 2004). Attempts at last-minute negotiation are also thwarted, as it is difficult to argue with a piece of paper or an object. The student learns to transition independently and to navigate his day without constant verbal prompting from adults (Mesibov *et al.*, 2004).

Schedules can be created using, in order of symbolic complexity: functional objects, representational objects, photographs, line drawings, written words, or a combination of these (Mesibov *et al.*, 2004). Combining these modes of presentation (e.g. taping line drawings to objects used in an object schedule) can ease the progression from one level to the next. In fact, we always use line drawings that have the written word on them for this reason. When deciding what kind of visual schedule to use with a student, we must assess where the student is functioning on this hierarchy of symbolic ability. We need to know that student is truly able to make the connection between the type of icon we are using and the activity it represents. Many of the students in our classroom can learn to use a schedule made with line drawings. However, it is not uncommon for us to begin with objects or photographs when teaching a student how to use a schedule.

There are several types of schedule that we use in our classroom. Many of our students use individual schedules to structure the whole preschool day. Some of our students also have visual schedules for particularly challenging or unstructured portions of the day (e.g. free-choice time, outside time). Finally, we have static schedules permanently posted throughout the classroom for some common routines to clarify the steps needed to complete them (e.g. arrival routine, hand washing, using the bathroom).

DAILY SCHEDULE

For the purposes of this explanation, we will describe a schedule made with line drawings, as this is the most commonly used type of schedule in our classroom. To make the schedule, we typically use a long, laminated piece of construction paper, with the icons attached using Velcro. As with all visual schedules, the icons are attached in order either from top to bottom or left to right, to support the development of literacy skills. The schedule is then posted where it is accessible to the student, with a clear indication that it is his schedule (e.g. color-coded, labeled with the student's name or photograph). An exception to this is when a student is learning the schedule, or is having difficulty transitioning to and from the schedule location, making it beneficial for the schedule to travel with him.

It is essential that the daily visual schedule system includes a transition object or a card that directs the student back to his schedule (Hume, n.d.). We often use a small laminated card that says, "check schedule," but any card or small object could be used for this purpose. The key is that the item successfully and reliably cues the student to return to his schedule. Customizing this aspect of the schedule is a great way to incorporate a student's interests to encourage willing participation. For example, each transition card could have a sticker or small drawing of a preferred item on it, such as a train or superhero. We must be careful, though, that the item captures the student's interest without distracting him from the task at hand. The system must include an envelope, pocket, or container in which the student places the transition item before checking his schedule. This receptacle is placed to the left of the visual schedule.

Figure 11.1 Daily visual schedule

Finally, for each picture on the student's schedule, there must be an exact match posted at the desired destination, on a piece of furniture or a wall near the activity or center. For example, if circle time is an item on the student's schedule, there must be a matching circle time icon posted on the wall near where this activity takes place. Note that when several students in the classroom are on daily schedules, there must be an icon available for each student at each location, again designated by color, name, or photo of student.

To implement the schedule, an adult gives the transition item to the student. This item directs the student to his schedule. Once the student is at his schedule, he puts the transition item in the envelope or container that is placed to the left of his schedule for this purpose. He then takes the next icon in line off the schedule, which directs him to his next activity. Once he arrives at the activity, the student matches his icon, attaching it to the identical picture (again, we use Velcro) stationed at the activity. As soon as the activity is complete, the adult who is working with the student must have the student's transition item ready to hand to the student, enabling him to transition smoothly back to his schedule.

An object schedule can be used with concrete learners who do not yet have the symbolic ability to associate a picture with the activity that it represents (Mesibov *et al.*, 2004). For students who need an object schedule, the objects used can be either functional or representational. A functional object is an object that will be used in the activity, such as a bottle of soap that the student will use to wash his hands when he arrives at the sink. This is the most concrete level of representation and may help the student make the cognitive connection required to comprehend symbol systems (Mesibov *et al.*, 2004). A representational object is slightly higher on the hierarchy, as it is an object that represents the activity, but will not be used as part of the activity. An example of this would be an empty bottle of soap that represents hand washing but will not actually be used in the process.

Often, we need to begin by teaching the student that the object represents the activity. When doing this, we give the objects to the student one at a time and guide him to the appropriate location. To encourage independence, we guide the student from behind, with hand-over-hand to hold the object, if necessary. The object is used as a transition item to take the student to the next activity, and we would typically begin with a functional object. Once the student clearly understands that the object represents the activity, we can attach the objects to a Velcro strip, just as we would with a picture schedule. Once a student masters the object schedule, we move him either to a photo schedule or a line-drawing schedule (as outlined above). A schedule using photographs of the actual activities within the classroom is the next step up from objects, regarding symbolic complexity, and may be the easiest for the student to understand. However, we have found that many students are ready to move straight to line drawings once they have mastered the object schedule.

UNSTRUCTURED TIME

It is well documented that students with ASD have significant difficulty coping with unstructured time. The unpredictability and lack of boundaries during these times can be anxiety-producing for our students (Mesibov *et al.*, 2004). Most preschool classrooms have free-choice time when students may choose which activity they would like to engage in and may flow freely from one area to another within the classroom. This part of the day is often an overwhelming time for students with autism. There are not only many choices to make, but also the classroom can be loud and chaotic. We use a choice board type of schedule during this time with many of our students, to add structure and predictability. Using this schedule will help each student organize himself, which not only supports regulation, but also makes choice-making more purposeful (Mesibov *et al.*, 2004). The choice board should be individualized for each student according to his functional level. For a student with the ability to scan visually and process many items at once, the board may present pictures of many options. For the student who is just learning the system, or does not have the cognitive ability to process more than a few choices, the visual schedule may show only two or three pictures at a time. As with the daily schedule, a choice board can be presented using objects or photos, as well as line drawings.

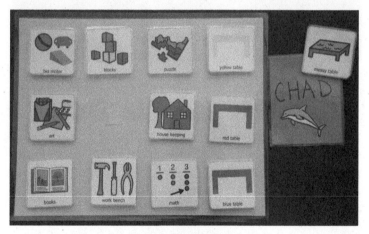

Figure 11.2 Choice board

The set-up for this type of schedule in our classroom includes the choice board, a laminated name card for each student with a small piece of Velcro in a top corner, and a sign at each activity that includes Velcro spots for the name cards (corresponding to the number of students allowed at each activity), an enlarged exact match of picture/activity icon, and an "All Done" pocket.

Figure 11.3 Matching sign at the activity

To implement this type of schedule, the student is presented with the choice board at the appropriate time in the daily schedule. He makes a choice and pulls the icon off the choice board, placing it onto the Velcro spot on his name card. He then carries his choice board and his name card to the activity, placing the name card (with the activity icon attached) on one of the available Velcro spots. He can place his choice board nearby and begin to play. Once the student is finished at that activity, he then takes his picture off his name card and puts it in the "All Done" pocket. He chooses the next activity icon from the choice board, attaches the picture to his name card, and proceeds to the next activity.

Outside time is another portion of the day that lacks structure. Many of our students don't know what to do outside, so they end up walking the perimeter of the playground alone or engaging in perseverative tasks. We have used several different types of visual schedules to structure outside time for our students. One student had photographs of outside activity choices on a ring that he could flip through and choose an activity from. Another student had an icon schedule of activities that he needed to complete in order, with some free time at the end. Still another, who tended to perseverate on going down the slide alone, had a chart to show how many times he could engage in that activity before moving on to something else or inviting a peer to join him. In fact, we always include activities that involve social interaction as items on schedules for outside time. It is not uncommon for us to witness our students with autism first interacting with peers when they are engaged in outdoor play, so we want to build on that tendency as much as possible.

INDIVIDUAL ACTIVITIES

As previously mentioned, static schedules can be permanently posted throughout the classroom to clarify the sequenced steps of common classroom routines (e.g. arrival routine, hand washing, using the bathroom). We have these schedules posted throughout the classroom so that we can refer the student to them when they are stuck, rather than using a lot of language to prompt them through the process. For students who need it, we can provide this same type of schedule with icons that can be removed as each step is completed and placed in an "All Done" envelope.

TIPS FOR TEACHING SCHEDULE USE

It's very important to remember that schedules will not be intuitive to a student initially. We need to *teach* the student how to use the visual schedule. When teaching the use of a visual schedule it may be important to include only two or three items at a time. This will give the student time to gain an understanding of the sequential way a schedule is used. It may also be helpful to begin with preferred activities, as the flow from one activity to the next is likely to be fluid, perhaps making this aspect of using the schedule more appealing and salient to the student. Most importantly, when teaching the use of a visual schedule, it's essential to use very little language—almost none. You are teaching him how to use the symbols, not how to follow verbal directions. The goal is for the schedule to guide the student, eliminating the need for teacher prompting and increasing student independence. The less we have inserted ourselves as part of the process, the easier that will be.

Eventually, some students with autism may not need a visual schedule, and the use of this type of support can be faded. However, as they are visual learners, many students with autism will continue to need some kind of visual schedule into adulthood. This is fine, as, in fact, many people need visual supports and schedules, such as daily "to-do" lists and calendars, throughout their lives. The key is for the level and type of visual support to grow and evolve with the student. Educators should always be careful to create visual schedules that are appropriate for the student's age and cognitive level. One student may need to continue with a stationary icon schedule, while another might work best with his schedule in a three-ring binder, while still another might successfully use a written list on a clipboard carried with him. It is important that, no matter how the schedule is implemented, it must be designed so that the student can use the schedule on his most difficult day (Hume, n.d.). The goal is independence and, as always, regulation and availability for learning.

▨ EXAMPLES

- Your student has difficulty following the daily classroom routine. He frequently wanders off, and does not seem aware that the rest of the class is following a set routine. He has frequent meltdowns when it is time to move from one activity to another within the daily routine. You know that he has the symbolic ability to know that line drawings can represent objects and activities. You set up a daily schedule for him using picture icons and begin teaching him how to use it. You know he particularly loves race cars and the color red, so you use cards with a picture of a red race car as his transition item.

- Your student is completely dependent upon adults to physically guide him from one activity to another during free choice time. He does not know that he is able to choose an activity on his own, and is not yet able to follow a verbal direction to go to a named activity/location within the room. He does not have the symbolic ability to understand that a picture can represent an object/activity in the real world. You set up an object schedule for him using functional objects (e.g. a wooden block that he carries to the block center and then uses for building) and begin to teach him how to use it. You start by guiding him from behind and helping him to hold the transition object in front of him, so that he can begin to see that the object helps him know where to go.

- Your student is not able to initiate or complete the hand-washing sequence without constant verbal prompting. He does not yet have the symbolic ability to comprehend line drawings, but knows that photographs can represent objects/activities in his world. You create a hand-washing sequence using photos and post it above the sink. You teach him how to use it by pointing to the photos and demonstrating the sequence. In future, you can simply gesture toward the photo sequence when your student gets stuck.

VISUAL SCHEDULES

Rationale

- ✓ Decrease anxiety; increase regulation
- ✓ Promote independence and flexibility
- ✓ Support visual learning style

Basic Considerations

- ✓ Arrange from right to left or top to bottom
- ✓ Include a transition item
- ✓ Incorporate the student's interests

Types of Visual Schedules

- ✓ Object, photo, line drawing, written
- ✓ Full day/partial day
- ✓ Unstructured time, common routines

Teaching Tips

- ✓ Very little talking
- ✓ Keep the schedule in the student's view, not the adult's
- ✓ Begin with two to three items when needed
- ✓ The schedule can travel with the student

ONE MORE THING

CHAPTER 12

TECHNIQUES

Over the years, we have acquired several techniques that enhance the effectiveness of the strategies we use with our students. The earlier chapters presented *what* to do to enhance regulation (the strategies), as well as discussion of *why* these are effective with students on the spectrum. This chapter will focus on some verbal and nonverbal techniques that we use that enhance *how* we interact with our students.

THINGS WE DO

Expectant look—Every educator who works with students on the spectrum should develop a good expectant look (eyes wide, eyebrows lifted). We use this while waiting for the student to respond to a direction and/or complete a task that we know he knows how to do. We often combine this with a deliberate gaze shift toward the task to be completed. We may also pair it with a gesture (e.g. point or tap) to clarify the expectation as needed.

Avert eyes—There are a couple of situations in which we would avert our eyes or avoid giving eye contact. One is when the student is having a tantrum. We don't want to reinforce the behavior by giving it a lot of attention. Of course, when the student is in a state of extreme dysregulation, we stay near him to provide emotional support and safety. And we certainly employ our strategies to assist the student in returning to a regulated state. However, we avoid looking directly at him as much as possible until he begins to regain control.

Another situation in which we would avert our eyes is when we are trying to entice the student to do something he is reluctant to do. Perhaps we want him to complete a puzzle and he is refusing or protesting. Once we have employed one or more of our strategies to give the activity structure (e.g. "Three puzzle pieces, then all done"), we could hold out the first puzzle piece (or move it toward the student) and wait without looking directly at him. This gives him the emotional space to relent and complete an activity that is not on his agenda. Looking straight at him is more confrontational and is likely to result in a power struggle.

Silent point—We use this very frequently throughout the day to let our students know what they should be attending to, without using a lot of language. For example, circle time can be very challenging for our students. There are many distractions, and sitting still can be challenging. With so much competing stimuli, it can be difficult for students with autism to know what they should attend to. So, we simply provide a silent point from behind the student toward the teacher. We typically point toward the teacher's face with our arm extended next to the student's face at eye level, and then direct our gaze toward the teacher's face as well.

Gently move hand/object down—This is a technique we use when we want to redirect a student's attention away from a sensory behavior without calling a lot of attention to it. For example, a student might frequently wave his fingers next to his eye to provide visual input to stay regulated. While this is regulating for the student, it also gets in the way of him attending to the people in his environment. Perhaps the student is doing this at circle time when we want him to attend to the teacher. We might silently and gently push his hand down to his lap and then follow that with a silent point to the teacher. We would also seek an alternate sensory behavior that might serve the same purpose for the student without affecting his ability to attend.

Pass hand in front of eyes/get in line of vision—Students with autism frequently become distracted by objects, patterns of light, parts of their own bodies, etc., both up close and at a distance. Similarly, they may become internally distracted, causing them to "stare into space." When the distraction is near the student's face or he is staring into space, we might simply pass a hand in front of the eyes to break the student's focus and then redirect his gaze toward the desired point of focus. When the distraction is further away, we might stand in the student's line of view and/or place a mat there if that distraction is a recurring one.

Hold both hands—We do this when we are waiting for a student to look at us, perhaps during a greeting or a request. When we hold both of the student's hands, it positions his body toward us and cues him to turn his head/face toward us as well. Of course, we would get on the student's level first, then hold both hands, and wait without calling his name or repeating the direction or greeting. Similarly, when a student is trying to give/take an object without eye gaze, we will hold the object, together with the student's hand, and wait for eye gaze. We should note here that, while we want to teach this skill, and work to give the student every opportunity to provide eye gaze (e.g. holding both hands, getting on their level, *waiting*, immediately responding when eye gaze is given), we do not insist on it. Communication can be directed in many ways including verbally, with touch, proximity, and eye gaze. We let the situation and our knowledge of each student guide our expectations in this area.

Corral—We are often able to get a student to move in the desired direction by using our bodies to move him along—by getting right behind him and moving in the direction he needs to go. We also use this technique to prevent a student from veering off course by simply moving into his path when he starts to go the wrong way. We do this without any talking and without calling attention to the fact that we are intentionally directing the student. Corralling the student fosters independence, as it provides some guidance while still requiring the student to think about where he is going. Leading the student by the hand is vastly different, as the adult is doing all the thinking.

Brief touch prompt—We use this technique to get the student started quickly on a task or keep him going. We touch the student only as much as needed to begin the motor movement, and only after providing ample wait time to give him a chance to begin or continue on his own. For example, a quick, light touch to the back of the arm is often all that is needed to participate in dancing at circle time or begin the process of hanging up a coat. Of course, we provide prompts at all levels along the continuum throughout the day. We included this here because we use it much more often than more intrusive levels of prompting, and because, again, it still requires the student to do some of the thinking about what his body is doing.

THINGS WE SAY

"You do it"—We use this when a student with autism is trying to get someone else to do something for him that he can do for himself and/or when we have demonstrated a skill that we want him to try. For example, the student may be trying to grab our hand to zip his coat. If we know he has that skill, we might put his hand on the zipper and say, "You do it." Or, perhaps we are working on imitation of simple motor tasks with a student. We might clap three times and then say, "You do it."

"Keep going"—We use this phrase when a student has started an activity or routine and then stopped. This happens often with students with autism. They may become distracted by internal thoughts or external events. Or, they may lose track of what they are doing, due to difficulty with executive functioning. Whatever the case, the student may need a cue to keep going. Note that this is vastly different from telling the student what to do next. When we say, "Keep going," the student must think about what comes next (P. Rydell, personal communication, 2011). This fosters independence and decreases the tendency to become prompt-dependent.

"Finish"—This is an alternative to "Keep going," and can be used when the student gets stuck near the end of the activity. A simple "Finish" cues him that the task is not complete, while still requiring him to do the thinking for himself and recall what he needs to do (P. Rydell, personal communication, 2011).

"Uh uh"—We often use a quick "Uh uh" when a student is engaging in a behavior we want him to stop. A positive statement or gesture indicating what we *want* the student to do always follows "Uh uh." The phrase "Uh uh" is much less loaded and definitive than the word "No," while still serving a similar purpose. We believe that, when working with students with autism, you must have a clear way to let them know that you want them to discontinue a behavior.

Different tones of voice should be used in different situations. For example, a stern tone of voice should be used when uttering "Uh uh" when safety is an issue, such as when the student is beginning to climb on top of the table. At first, this would most likely be paired with full or partial physical assistance and followed with a simple "Feet down," or just "Down." A gentler tone of voice could be used in a situation where there is no danger involved, such as when the child is beginning to move away from what he is supposed to be doing. A quick, gentle "Uh uh," immediately followed by an indication of what he should be doing (e.g. a single word, point, corral in the right direction), can often get the student back on track.

"Shhh"—Said softly and soothingly, this is a very useful way to help settle the student when he is becoming distracted and slightly agitated/dysregulated. It is not used in the typical context of "Be quiet," but rather means re-focus and come back to what we're doing together. It is surprising how quickly students come to understand what this means. It is often very effective when paired with some calming sensory input, such as deep pressure on the arms.

STRATEGIES AT A GLANCE

- Model
- Show how many/show how long
- Verbalize a rule
- First/Then
- Offer a choice
- I start/you finish
- Simple tasks
- Incentive charts
- Visual schedules

TECHNIQUES AT A GLANCE

THINGS WE DO

Expectant look

- To encourage a response while waiting for the student to respond or complete a task

Avert eyes

- To decrease attention to behavior

- To decrease pressure when enticing a student to participate

Silent point

- To direct a student's attention to what is important

Gently move hand/object down

- To move a hand/object out of the student's line of vision

Pass hand in front of eyes/get in line of vision

- To interrupt the student's focus and redirect it towards what is important

Hold both hands

- To orient the student's body toward you and encourage eye gaze

Corral

- To help move the student in the appropriate direction without doing the thinking for him

Brief touch prompt

- To give the student a slight tactile cue to get a motor movement going

THINGS WE SAY

"You do it"

- To encourage a student to try something on his own

"Keep going"

- To prompt a student to keep going when he has stopped mid-stream

"Finish"

- To prompt a student to finish a task when he has stopped near the end

"Uh uh"

- To indicate that a behavior should be discontinued; follow with a statement of what the student *should* do

"Shhh"

- To help re-focus a student when he is becoming slightly distracted and agitated

APPENDIX C

SAMPLE GOALS

- _____ will respond to cognitive/language strategies to help him stay regulated (e.g. First/Then, modeling) in eight out of ten opportunities with no more than one repetition. Response must be timely (within 30 seconds) and occur before he reaches a state of extreme dysregulation.

- When provided with a visual support (e.g. choice board, video modeling, visual schedule), _____ will stay regulated and engaged during a _____ (individual, small group, large group) activity for _____ minutes 80 percent of the time.

- _____ will use language strategies to regulate his behavior to keep himself and others safe in _____ out of ten opportunities with _____ (verbal, gestural, visual) cues as needed.

- When becoming dysregulated, _____ will choose a calming strategy from a field of two (e.g. put-in, lazy eight breathing) in four out of five opportunities given _____ (maximum, moderate, minimum) cues.

• _____ will decrease the time needed to recover from extreme dysregulation to _____ minutes when provided with pictures, words, and/or sensory input from a familiar adult in four out of five opportunities.[1]

---

1   Adapted from The SCERTS Model goal MR4.4, SR4.4 (Prizant *et al.*, 2006).

SAMPLE SITUATIONS

This appendix will outline several possible classroom scenarios, along with some of the primary strategies we might use to support the student in each scenario. We will assume that in each situation you have already employed the Three Guidelines by making sure the student has had enough *time to process* the situation and that you have used *simple language* and *visuals* to structure the situation.

Situation 1: The student is becoming dysregulated during arrival when it is time to hang up his backpack.

Strategies

Model: Point out what the other students are doing, "Everyone is hanging up backpacks." Or model it yourself, while calling attention to what you are doing without a lot of language (e.g. "Backpack").

Verbalize a rule: "We all hang up backpacks at school."

First/Then: Pull out a First/Then visual, with an icon of a backpack under "First" and a picture representing a preferred activity (e.g. high-five or tickles) under "Then." Give a First/

Then such as "First backpack, then circle time," if that will be motivating for the student.

Offer a choice: Give the student a choice that fits within the expectation of hanging up his backpack (e.g. "Backpack first or coat?").

I start/you finish: Start hanging up the backpack hand-over-hand with the student. Back your hands away and let the student finish independently if possible.

Incentive chart: If hanging up the backpack is an ongoing issue and you know the student has the skills to do it, you can set up an incentive chart.

Visual schedule: It is a good idea to have a visual schedule of the classroom arrival routine permanently posted for all students. If needed, you can add an individual schedule for a student, perhaps adding a way for him to interact with the schedule, such as taking each picture off and putting it in an "all done" pocket as that step is completed.

Situation 2: The student is becoming dysregulated over washing his hands before a snack.

Strategies

Model: Provided the student is near the sink, you can wash your hands first and call attention to what you are doing. Better yet, call the student's attention to a peer who is washing his hands. If it is an ongoing problem based on difficulty in sequencing the activity, you can consider making a video of another child washing his hand. You would then show the video to the student before hand washing, calling attention to each step of the process. The video can be shown in segments and paused while the student completes each step, if necessary.

Show how many: Showing the student how many steps there are in the process by using a visual may be helpful. For example, point to three pictures in turn or hold up three fingers while you say, "Soap, water, towel, then all done."

Verbalize a rule: State a rule, "The rule is: wash hands before eating," or give a script, "I wash my hands before snack." Related to this would be singing a song while washing hands. This adds an element of fun and rhythm and may distract the child from his agenda long enough to get the hand-washing started.

First/Then: Simply state, "First wash hands, then snack." Provide a First/Then visual if necessary. Stop talking after you have stated the First/Then and gently guide the student from behind, if needed.

Offer a choice: "Wash hands in the bathroom or at the big sink?" or "Wash hands by yourself or together?" or "Foam soap or pink soap?"

I start/you finish: You start the process of hand washing together with the student (hand-over-hand) and then back off and let him finish on his own. Or just give the student a quick touch prompt (e.g. light touch to the back of the elbows to move the hands forward toward the faucet) to get the task started.

Incentive chart: If hand washing is an ongoing point of difficulty, you could create an incentive chart for this activity.

Visual schedule: Post a visual schedule of the hand-washing routine above the sink. We have this posted above all our sinks at all times, so all students can refer to it quickly and easily.

Situation 3: The student is becoming dysregulated because there has been a change to the schedule. It is snowing, so outside time has been replaced with inside play.

Strategies

Model: If the student has sufficient receptive language (and is only mildly dysregulated), you can express your disappointment over not going outside, as well as your flexibility around the change using simple language; "I'm disappointed. I love outside time. Oh well, maybe tomorrow." Remember to include pauses between ideas so that the student can process each chunk of language. Alternatively, you can point out how other students are handling the change.

Verbalize a rule: Not quite a rule, but a simple statement can be made before moving on; "Sometimes the schedule changes" or "Sometimes we do something different."

Offer a choice: You could try to distract the student and give him some control by giving him a choice; "We are playing inside. Art or messy table?"

I start/you finish: Entice and distract the student by starting an activity that is motivating and interesting to him, such as a marble run.

Simple task: Quickly providing a simple task (e.g. puzzle, put-in, etc.) may help the student stay regulated and process the change without a full meltdown.

Visual schedule: A visual of the daily schedule is always visible in our classroom for all students. This can be especially helpful for our students with autism. You can use it to show changes in the schedule by switching the order of the icons and/or swapping one icon for another. It is important to work on flexibility by making small changes to the schedule regularly. Another exercise to promote flexibility can be to have an icon that represents a "surprise" (we use a star). The teacher can put this in different places on the schedule and introduce any activity as the surprise.

Situation 4: The student is becoming dysregulated because he does not want to leave his favorite activity at free-choice time. He has been in that area for a long time and other students are waiting for a turn.

Strategies

Model: Point out another child who has been at that activity and is moving on amicably. "Jack is all done at messy table. He is going to blocks." You can even recruit the peer to invite your student along.

Show how many/show how long: Use a visual timer to give the student time to process the change, "Two more minutes, then choose a new activity." Leave the timer where the student can see it but cannot touch it. Show him the timer when the time is up, and immediately present a choice of two activities.

Verbalize a rule: "The rule is: ten minutes at each activity." Use a visual timer if that is helpful.

First/Then: "*First* two more minutes. *Then* new activity," or "*First* messy table. *Then* blocks," if time isn't meaningful for the student.

Offer a choice: Give a choice of two preferred activities as above.

Simple task: There have been times when we have had a student for whom learning the process of transitioning from one area to another at free-choice time was particularly difficult. Often, providing the student with a simple task in the same spot (e.g. at the yellow table) between each activity can add structure to help him stay regulated and learn the process. This works well when paired with a visual schedule.

Incentive chart: If switching centers is an ongoing sticking point, and you have tried several other strategies without success, you can create an incentive chart. The student would receive a sticker/icon each time he moved on without incident.

Visual schedule: Many of our students are on visual schedules for center time. Free-choice time is one of the more unstructured times of the day, and the visual schedule helps add structure. When giving a choice of a new area, use the icons to support comprehension and make the task clear.

REFERENCES

American Psychiatric Association (2013). *Diagnostic and Statistical Manual of Mental Disorders* (5th ed.). Washington, DC: American Psychiatric Association.

Amos, P. (2013). 'Rhythm and timing in autism: Learning to dance.' *Frontiers in Integrative Neuroscience, 7.* Accessed on 28/09/17 at http://journal.frontiersin. org/article/10.3389/fnint.2013.00027/full.

Ball, J. (2008). *Early Intervention and Autism.* Arlington, TX: Future Horizons, Inc.

Bandura, A. (1977). *Social Learning Theory.* Englewood Cliffs, NJ: Prentice-Hall.

Baron-Cohen, S. (2001). 'Theory of mind in normal development and autism.' *Prisme 34,* 174–183.

Center for Disease Control and Prevention (2016). *Autism Spectrum Disorder (ASD) Data and Statistics.* Accessed on 28/09/17 at www.cdc.gov/ncbddd/autism/data. html.

Charlop-Christy, M. H., Le, L., and Freeman, K. A. (2000). 'A comparison of video modeling with in vivo modeling for teaching students with autism.' *Journal of Autism and Developmental Disorders 30,* 537–552.

Corbett, B. A. and Abdullah, M. (2005). 'Video modeling: Why does it work for students with autism?' *Journal of Early and Intensive Behavior Intervention 2,* 1.

Eckenrode, L., Fennell, P., and Hearsey, K. (2013). *Tasks Galore.* Raleigh, NC: Tasks Galore Publishing Inc.

Fox, L., Dunlap, G., Hemmeter, M. L., Joseph, G. E., and Strain, P. S. (2003). 'The teaching pyramid: A model for supporting social competence and preventing challenging behavior in young children.' *Young Children 58,* 4, 48–52.

Garland, T. (2014). *Self-Regulation Interventions and Strategies: Keeping the Body, Mind and Emotions on Task in Children with Autism, ADHD or Sensory Disorders.* Eau Claire, WI: PESI.

Gould, J. and Ashton-Smith, J. (2011). 'Missed diagnosis, or misdiagnosis? Girls and women on the autism spectrum.' *Good Autism Practice (GAP) 12,* 1, 34–41.

Griffin, W. and AFIRM Team (2017). *Scripting.* Chapel Hill, NC: National Professional Development Center on Autism Spectrum Disorder, FPG Child Development Center, University of North Carolina. Accessed on 28/09/17 at http://afirm. fpg.unc.edu/scripting.

Hodgdon, L. (1991). 'Solving behavior problems through better communication strategies.' *Autism Society of America Conference Proceedings.* Indianapolis.

Hodgdon, L. Q. (1995). 'Solving Social-Behavioral Problems Through the Use of Visually Supported Communication.' In K. A. Quill (ed.) *Teaching Children with Autism: Strategies to Enhance Communication and Socialization* (pp.265–286). New York, NY: Delmar Publishers Inc.

Hodgdon, L. A. (1999). *Solving Behavior Problems in Autism: Improving Communication with Visual Strategies.* Troy, MI: QuirkRoberts.

Hume, K. (n.d.). *Structured Teaching Strategies: A Series.* Accessed on 28/09/17 at www. iidc.indiana.edu/pages/Structured-Teaching-Strategies-A-Series.

Janzen, J. E. and Zenko, C. B. (2012). *Understanding the Nature of Autism: A Guide to the Autism Spectrum Disorders* (3rd ed.). Austin, TX: Hamill Institute on Disabilities.

Joseph, G. E. and Strain, P. S. (2004). 'Building positive relationships with young children.' *Young Exceptional Children 7*, 4, 21–28.

Kaiser, B. and Rasminsky, J. S. (2012). *Challenging Behavior in Young Children: Understanding, Preventing, and Responding Effectively* (3rd ed.). Upper Saddle River, NJ: Pearson.

Kana, R. K., Keller, T. A., Cherkassky, V. L., Minshew, N. J, and Just, M. A. (2006). 'Sentence comprehension in autism: Thinking in pictures with decreased functional connectivity.' *Brain 129*, 2484–2493.

Koegel, R. L. and Koegel, L. K. (2006). *Pivotal Response Treatments for Autism: Communication, Social, and Academic Development.* Baltimore, MD: Paul H. Brookes Publishing Co.

Kranowitz, C. S. (2006a). *The Out-Of-Sync Child Has Fun: Activities for Kids with Sensory Processing Disorder.* New York, NY: Perigree.

Kranowitz, C. S. (2006b). *The Out-Of-Sync Child: Recognizing and Coping with Sensory Processing Disorder.* Revised edition. New York, NY: Perigree.

Lowry, L. (2016). *What is Behaviour Regulation? And What Does It Have To Do With Language Development?* Accessed on 28/09/17 at www.hanen.org/helpful-info/ articles/what-is-behaviour-regulation--and-what-does-it-hav.aspx.

MacDuff, G. S., Krantz, P. J., and McClannahan, L. E. (1993). 'Teaching children with autism to use photographic activity schedules: Maintenance and generalization of lengthy response chains.' *Journal of Applied Behavior Analysis 26*, 1, 89–97.

Mesibov, G. B., Shea, V., and Schopler, E. (2004). *The TEACCH Approach to Autism Spectrum Disorders.* New York, NY: Springer.

Miller, L. J. (2014). *Sensational Kids: Hope and Help for Children with Sensory Processing Disorder (SPD).* New York, NY: Perigree.

National Professional Development Center on Autism Spectrum Disorder (n.d.). *What are Evidence-Based Practices?* Accessed on 28/09/17 at http://autismpdc.fpg.unc. edu/evidence-based-practices.

National Research Council (2001). 'Educating Children with Autism.' In C. Lord and James P. McGee (eds) *Committee on Educational Interventions for Children with Autism.* Washington, DC: National Academy Press.

Premack, D. (1965). 'Reinforcement Theory.' In D. Levine (ed.), *Nebraska Symposium on Motivation* (Vol. 13, pp. 123-188). Lincoln: University of Nebraska Press.

Prizant, B. M. and Laurent, A. (2011a). 'Behavior is not the issue: An emotional regulation perspective on problem behavior, Part One.' *Autism Spectrum Quarterly, Spring*, 28-30.

Prizant, B. M. and Laurent, A. (2011b). 'Behavior is not the issue: An emotional regulation perspective on problem behavior, Part Two.' *Autism Spectrum Quarterly, Summer*, 34–37.

Prizant, B. M. and Laurent, A. C. (2014). 'On earning.' *Autism Spectrum Quarterly, Fall,* 46–48.

Prizant, B. M. and Meyer, E. (1993). 'Socioemotional aspects of language and social-communication disorders in young children and their families.' *American Journal of Speech-Language Pathology, 2,* 56.

Prizant, B. M., Wetherby, A. M., Rubin, E., Laurent, A. C., and Rydell, P. J. (2006). *The SCERTS Model: A Comprehensive Educational Approach for Children with Autism Spectrum Disorders.* Baltimore, MD: Paul H. Brookes Publishing Co.

Quill, K. A. (1997). 'Instructional considerations for young children with autism: The rationale for visually cued instructions.' *Journal of Autism and Developmental Disorders 21,* 697–714.

Reeve, C. E. and Kabot, S. S. (2012). *Building Independence: How to Create and Use Structured Work Systems.* Shawnee Mission, KS: AAPC Publishing.

Rydell, P. J. (n.d.). *Learning Style Profile: Are We Interference?* Accessed on 28/09/17 at www.rockymountainautismcenter.com/site/files/1061/145770/482907/734758/Learning_Style_Profile-_Are_We_Interference_.pdf.

Rydell, P. J. (2012). *Learning Style Profile for Children with Autism Spectrum Disorders.* [Mobile application software.] Accessed on 28/09/17 at https://itunes.apple.com/us/book/learning-style-profile-for-children-autism-spectrum/id582146281?mt=11.

Sam, A. and AFIRM Team. (2015). *Functional Behavior Assessment.* Chapel Hill, NC: National Professional Development Center on Autism Spectrum Disorder, FPG Child Development Center, University of North Carolina. Accessed on 28/09/17 at http://afirm.fpg.unc.edu/functional-behavior-assessment.

Schuler, A. L. (1995). 'Thinking in Autism: Differences in Learning and Development.' In K. A. Quill (ed.) *Teaching Children with Autism: Strategies to Enhance Communication and Socialization* (pp.11–32). New York, NY: Delmar.

The SCERTS Model (2017). *Frequently Asked Questions.* Accessed on 28/09/17 at www.scerts.com/index.php?option=com_content&view=article&id=5&Itemid=5.

Williams, D. L. and Minshew, N. J. (2010). 'How the brain thinks in autism.' *The ASHA Leader 15,* 5, 8–11.

Winner, M. G. (2007). *Thinking About You, Thinking About Me: Teaching Perspective Taking and Social Thinking to Persons with Social Cognitive Learning Challenges* (2nd Ed.). San Jose, CA: Think Social Publishing, Inc.

Winner, M. G. and Abildgaard, C. (2010). 'The next generation of treatment: Defining a hybrid of social interventions for students with strong intelligence and language skills.' *Autism Asperger's Digest 28-31,* 68.

Winner, M. G. and Crooke, P. (2013). *ABA and Social Thinking: Summary of a talk given by Dr. Joanne Gerenser and Michelle G. Winner at ASHA 2013.* [Course summary.] San Jose, CA: Think Social Publishing.

Wiseman, D. G. and Hunt, G. (2008). *Best Practice in Motivation and Management in the Classroom.* Springfield, IL: Charles C. Thomas Publisher.

World Health Organization (2017). *Autism Spectrum Disorders.* Accessed on 28/09/17 at www.who.int/mediacentre/factsheets/autism-spectrum-disorders/en.

INDEX